PRAISE FOR FAULT LINES

Bishop Pitts takes a deep dive into an area seldom excavated by a clergy. His book aides us to process those unpredictable moments in our lives, when the tremors of heartbreak, disaster, human frailty and tragic events, result in an earthquake for the soul. I simply don't know anyone who has escaped those moments. Therefore, this is a book that you will need or have needed in order to be on the survivors list of life.

T. D. Jakes Sr., Senior Pastor, The Potter's House of Dallas, Inc. /
TDJ Enterprises, New York Times best-selling Author

Fault lines. That one word conjures pictures of imminent calamity. However in his book Fault lines my friend, Michael Pitts, helps us understand that we don't have to succumb to fault lines. Even as importantly Fault lines encourages us that there is recovery from the disaster we might have experienced—before the earthquakes and after we're covered with debris and even if others including ourselves have given up on us. This book will reach back for you if you have experienced disasters and reach forward into your life even as you prepare to deal with Fault lines. You'll read, learn, be encouraged and send gifts of this book to all you care for.

Sam Chand, Leadership Consultant and author
of Leadership Pain

Bishop Michael Pitts is one of the most articulate, passionate, and prophetic voices I know. His ability to combine Biblical soundness and prophetic insight with cultural critique is notable and worth paying attention to. Today we face chaotic and rapid change due to the tectonic plates of culture being shaken. The impact of which is felt at the fault lines of every community, city, nation, and the nations of the world. Those fault lines are the front lines of our spiritual pilgrimage and warfare. In the midst of knowing that everything that can be shaken, will be shaken, Bishop Pitts masterfully takes us to a place where we can learn how to remain grounded in a Kingdom that cannot be shaken in Christ Jesus. Listen well as you read this masterful exegesis of the current hour.

Bishop Mark J. Chironna, Church On The Living Edge

There are hundreds maybe thousands of books written about how to win the lost, but very few about how to retrieve, retain, and restore the found. I love the perspective of Bishop Michael Pitts in identifying the need and giving us an exceptional set of tools to navigate the storms of life. I'm grateful for him and this amazing life changing book.

Israel Houghton, Six time Grammy® Winner &
Eleven time Dove Award Winner

Without a doubt, one of the most prolific and passionate voices in the Kingdom of God today, my brother and dear friend Bishop Michael Pitts once again equips the church with a life-changing truth; "Fault Lines".

In this book you will learn to build a firewall against constant breaking while simultaneously acquiring the anointing and spiritual empowerment to shake off whatever life and hell sends your way. This is beyond a "must read" this is a "must do!"

Samuel Rodriguez, Founder and Pastor, New Season Christian Worship
Center / President of the National Hispanic Christian
Leadership Conference

Cataloging-in-Publication Data is available from the
Library of Congress
ISBN 978-1-7329003-0-1 (hardcover)
ISBN 978-1-7329003-1-8 (ebook)

For more information, speaking engagements and additional product
visit: www.michaelpitts.com
PO Box 351690 • Toledo, OH 43635

FAULT LINES

THINGS THAT SHAKE YOU DON'T HAVE TO BREAK YOU

MICHAEL PITTS

ACKNOWLEDGMENTS

Thanks to those who through many conversations and exchanges helped in clarifying my thoughts in Fault Lines including: Kim Butler (Pathways Christian Counseling) and Theresa M. Abec, PCC. Thanks to Joshua Cunning for the cover design and book layout. Thank you Leah Parker for your patience in editing yet another book.

To those who are resilient survivors, who continue to stand and help others do the same.

TABLE OF CONTENTS

INTRODUCTION

Life is lived on levels and experienced in seasons. Through decades of ministry, I have witnessed and walked with those traversing shaky terrain. Some quakes were self-imposed and some we did not see coming.

Through those times, I have been both navigator and negotiator, navigating through difficult days and negotiating on behalf of those who needed to rebuild what their life-quake destroyed.

I am convinced that the power to bounce back is resident in the human heart. Resiliency is a great commodity. My desire is for you to win. I hope this writing helps.

CHAPTER 1
THE LIFE-QUAKE

Somewhere in the middle, it happens. In mid-stride, in the middle of the hustle and bustle of our lives, it strikes. It is the *life-quake* − the sudden, seismic shift in the landscape of our lives that exposes the cracks in our foundation and reveals the integrity of our supporting structures. It is the arrow that flies at noon-day, when the sun is at its peak. It springs up in trouble and in trauma, empowered by the unresolved, the pain of the past, and the existential angst churning just beneath the surface. Without invitation, announcement, or apology, it hits.

Much like its geological counterpart, the earthquake, the life-quake makes us feel as though nothing is stable and there is nowhere to run. Established structures of thought and emotion sway. Ethics and values strain to maintain their integrity. Relationships under its seismic grip feel the pressure of avoiding total collapse.

In the aftermath, we take inventory. We count the bodies and mourn the losses, amazed at the stories of those who survived and disheartened at the realization that others did not. Accounts of heroism emerge from first responders and regular citizens alike and give us a moment to catch our breath before the questions begin.

"Where were the warning signs?"
"Did we build properly?"
"Did we have a plan … just in case?"

The truth is, right in the middle of our journey, in the middle of the life and legacy we are building, conditions for the perfect storm are brewing. When the life-quake strikes, it is because the ground we are building on has begun to move, and the devastation that follows reveals that we have been living and building on fault lines all along.

Fault lines are the unstable beliefs and values we build our lives on, expecting certain outcomes. When we find our value system shifting with age and experience, the unsettling feeling that what we *were* pursuing is not what we are *now* pursuing produces a chasm between what we once thought and what we now think.

We can all identify with the shock of seeing a life-quake strike those who had built lives filled with impressive achievement. I am not alone in the numbing bewilderment that accompanies the news that some "great one," a hero, whom we have known intimately or from a distance, has fallen. "They seemed to be doing so well," we think. "I had no idea," we say.

I believe there is something in common among everyone I have ever known to experience this quake that results in crashing and burning. Quite simply, none of them ever set out to crash and burn.

No one starts a journey to get lost. No bride or groom walks down the aisle on their big day with a break-up in mind. No one crafts and cultivates the occasion with the intention of severing that celebrated union somewhere down the road. What parents ever gaze into the eyes of their newborn child, strategizing about how to so strain that bond that only bitterness and resentment return their gaze in the future? Businesses are started with dreams of "making it big" and attaining financial independence. We're motivated in those early days of envisioning the great success we'll achieve by the hopes of being our own boss and leaving a legacy for our children. We certainly don't plan on losing our life savings and spending years trying to recover from financial ruin. The young evangelist, the interim pastor, the rising singer, when answering "the call," did it with fear and trembling. They didn't plan on crashing and burning.

Knowing that no one plans to experience devastation, this critical question is revealed: Did we plan *not* to?

An older gentleman who was dying prematurely once said to me, "By the time I figured out what life was about, it was time to say good-bye."

Sadness and discouragement accompany tragic loss, along with the sobering reminder that none of us is immune to experiencing a life-quake. No one is invisible or hidden from its reach. Everyone gets weary and we all have the potential to burn out. Life-quakes are unimpressed by titles. They don't check our zip codes or calendars. They don't discriminate by race or gender or by whether we're rich or poor. The familiar house built on the sand and the house built on the rock (see Matthew 7:24-27) both experienced the same storm.

Knowing that these quakes can happen to any of us, we need to know there is hope. We can learn how to recognize the fault lines lying just beneath the surface in ourselves and others. We can learn how to rebuild and reinforce the structures of our lives to withstand the inevitable shifts and shaking. Ultimately, restoration is possible, and I believe that, while we cannot avoid all trouble or transition, we can emerge from devastation stronger than before.

An earthquake occurs when the surface of the earth shifts due to stored stress along faults or points of weakness just beneath the surface. When the stress below the surface exceeds the strength of the layers above, these layers fracture along a fault line, creating intense waves and violent shaking.

San Francisco, 1906

In the United States of America, no other fault line is more famous, more well-known, than the San Andreas Fault, stretching 750 miles through the state of California. Its prominence emerged in the great San Francisco earthquake of 1906.

The energy of the city of San Francisco at the turn of the century was palpable. Just walking through the streets, you could see people from all over the world and hear languages unfamiliar at that time to most Americans. Trolley cars clanged their way through the city while merchants set up shop in storefronts and stands along the street. In the morning, enticing scents wafted out of famous bakeries, carried along by the breeze off the bay.

However busy its residents were, though, the pace at which they moved belied the reality that, just under the surface of their city, tectonic plates were moving ever so slightly. No one had given much thought, really, to the fact that this city was built along a fault line. And, as it goes with fault lines, it is not a matter of *if* the ground will shake, but only *when*.

In the early dawn hours on April 18, 1906, the San Andreas fault succumbed to the pressure beneath the surface, and a massive earthquake shook the residents of San Francisco and leveled the city. What followed was even more devastating, as broken gas lines ignited fires throughout the area, causing more damage than the quake itself. Casualties reached the thousands, and the event left more than half of the population of this shattered city homeless.[1] It remains one of the nation's deadliest disasters.

Often, the things that consume our time and energy are the things that are seen on the surface of our lives. Our activities, hobbies, work pursuits, and social status give the appearance of a life that is well-ordered, structured, stable, and satisfying. Yet, over time, the values we have built our lives on inevitably begin to shift. Some things rise to greater importance and priority while others shift downward. In the midst of building our lives on these seemingly steady structures, we come face-to-face with our own life-quakes – tragedy, trauma, or transition – and then we begin to tremble. When these hit us, our lives shake and our foundations crack. Many times, the damage is not all immediate, but the aftershocks that follow create a ripple effect that exposes a life built on a fault line.

Some people withstand these quakes and even come out better, having been able to shore up cracks in their foundation, while others tragically succumb to the devastation. Never figuring out how to rebuild, they crash and burn, bailing on

1 "Casualties and Damage after the 1906 Earthquake." USGS: Science for a Changing World. https://earthquake.usgs.gov/earthquakes/events/1906calif/18april/casualties.php (accessed October 1, 2017).

a lifetime of relationships and achievements because of the destructive disillusionment that produced their internal quake.

The familiar "mid-life crisis" is one example of a life-quake, but the truth is, it can happen at varying places along the timeline of a person's life. Whenever we have competing values and ethics that begin to move under the surface of our lives, we find that the integrity of what and how we have built is tested.

CHAPTER 2
HOW DID WE GET HERE?

J.T.'s Story

After humble and uncertain beginnings, J.T. had found success. As he sat with me over lunch, he relayed several things. His bills were paid – mostly. His family was intact – mostly. His ministry and church were moving forward, positioned for greatness – mostly. When I use this word "mostly," I mean he had passed through those early stages of survival and had resources available to meet his needs. But, under the surface was an unsettledness and an uneasiness. Something was eating and gnawing at him, even on a subconscious level. But, what was it? Why was he unhappy and not at peace? He couldn't find the articulation for this nagging frustration.

I listened for patterns, thoughts, perceptions, and feelings. In observing tone, micro-expressions, body language, pace, and pathos, I found his real story. It was laced with accomplishments. His new home had been built, his church was nearly paid for, and he had many important people who looked up to him. I was struck by the feeling that his description was not about bragging, but it was simply an indication of his value system.

I became aware that something was missing. He didn't have the spark in his eyes or the animation you would associate with someone who was describing being "on top." His affect wasn't flat, but it was unconvincing.

Eventually, I asked him, "If everything is going so well, why did you come to see me?" That's when he broke. The walls he had built up began to come down. His defenses dropped and the tears began to flow. Then came his reply, "I'm lost. I don't know what I'm doing and I don't know where I'm going."

In that moment, I realized that J.T., like so many of us, was experiencing a shaking, a mid-journey life-quake. His fault lines were emerging and the tectonic plates of his belief systems were moving. His internal house was crumbling.

Daniel's Story

Daniel was the owner of a vibrant and successful Italian restaurant. He was large, gregarious, and filled the room not only with his size but also with his personality. He had started his restaurant in his mid-20s, offering up Old World recipes and a few of his own creations. He had built a steady clientele of upscale patrons. If you didn't call ahead and make a reservation, you didn't get a table.

Part of the attraction was that every hour, on the hour, Daniel would stand in the middle of the restaurant and sing opera at the top of his lungs. He was quite good, and it made for something you wouldn't get anywhere else.

I struck up a conversation with Daniel, who was in his

late 40s/early50s by this time and, in short order, found him experiencing a life-quake. He had, at one time, owned both a Porsche and a Ferrari, lived in a multimillion-dollar home, and had enough bling to make most rappers jealous.

As our conversation progressed, he volunteered that in the last year, he had sold both of his cars and his house, he and his wife were divorcing, and he was scaling down his business. I asked him what he was doing with himself and he replied, "I am traveling for the first time." He had taken a month off, jumped on a motorcycle, and went on a road trip. He came back, worked for another month, and then took another few weeks off.

I was hearing in his story the regret of having spent so much time accumulating things that he had forgotten how to live. The problem was, he had built his world on a belief system that he no longer adhered to. As he began to age a bit, he found that you can only drive one car at a time. He became less concerned with what he was driving than where he was going. He found that he had no time to visit places he had only read about. He had little time to devote to his internal world or to his wife and kids, and soon the emptiness inside him could not be filled by the square footage of his house or be satisfied by the roar of the Ferrari's engine. Staying busy was his drug. It kept him numb to the small tremors happening around him and to the feeling that the ground beneath his feet was moving.

When his childhood friend received a terminal diagnosis and lived only a few short weeks thereafter, the tectonic plates under Daniel's world shifted. He found himself seeking to make sense of what seemed to him a senseless existence – trying to figure out how it all went so wrong, trying to recapture seasons of youth, and trying to find a more carefree existence.

The casualties were Daniel's family and his marriage. The expensive and bitter divorce consumed most of their money and devoured several years of their children's youth.

Daniel finally closed his famous restaurant for good, perhaps to rid himself of the weight of management, or perhaps to spite his wife and escape alimony payments. I suppose the final casualties were those who frequented his Italian restaurant who would never again hear him sing.

Rachel's Story

Rachel loved her job. She interned at a high-powered technology company during her senior year of college. She quickly caught the eye and favor of one of the senior vice presidents, Nancy. Nancy had been there from the start and had helped to build the company up to become a recognized name in the industry. Perhaps because Rachel reminded her of herself – eager, capable, and hard-working – she took her under her wing, to mentor her and guide through the shark-infested waters of corporate politics.

For the next several years, Rachel had the time of her life. Although she and her friends occasionally bemoaned their lack of significant love lives, the truth is that they were more concerned with climbing the ladder than building a nest.

To say that Rachel worshipped Nancy would be an overstatement, but her feelings were somewhere north of admiration. To Rachel, she was an icon. She was everything that Rachel wanted to be. That is, until one fateful Friday.

Rachel had been scheduled to catch up with Nancy to fill her in on her latest project. But, when she stepped off the elevator on the executive floor, she found it eerily quiet. All the clerical workers were standing together and the hallway was filled with security personnel. Something was going on. As she stood there puzzled, it only took a moment until she saw Nancy being escorted out by two sheriffs with her hands cuffed behind her back.

News spread fast that the senior vice president had been embezzling funds. The elaborate scheme of fake contracts and bank accounts was not enough to shield her from the latest audit. All of these details aside, none of the facts or figures mattered to Rachel. The last images of Nancy being escorted past her shattered years of admiration. She certainly would not have believed the allegations to be true and would have defended Nancy's honor to the death had it not been for the words Nancy mouthed to her as she walked past: "I'm sorry."

Where is Here?

Our story is the narrative we tell others and the dialogue we have within ourselves. Somehow, over time, we craft a seamless internal biography, placing ourselves at the center. Our story has its villains, heroes, victims, and innocent bystanders. We highlight facts that reinforce our beliefs and values, and we quash mitigating and contradictory evidence. This truth is without judgment. It is what it is. Whether it is a survival mechanism, coping, denial, self-preservation, or selective memory is not my immediate point. Instead, I want you to see that your story remains real to you, and you can get stuck in the character role you have assigned yourself until you decide to change it.

Maybe the stories you just read are like your own, or maybe they are to you a collection of cautionary tales. Somewhere, hopefully, we have an epiphany. What we're driving is not as important as where we're going. What we're modeling in fashion is not as important as what we're modeling in our character – a good name on a label is not as important as a good name for ourselves.

We need to ask ourselves, "What does my next chapter look like? Who am I? How did I get here, and where exactly *is* here?"

The thing about time is that it changes our perspective. Aided by pressure and pain, and influenced by the unexpected twists and turns in the road we travel, we all inevitably end up with a "here." But, the realization of where we are is actually the beginning of progress. It's good to be able to look on the map of life's journey and see, "You are *here*."

I like the way the prophet Isaiah says it when receiving his commission in Isaiah 6:8 (NIV): "Here am I. Send me." Similar to what we see in Genesis 3:9, God, in effect, calls to each of us, "Adam, where are you?" It's not because God doesn't know. The question is meant to bring introspection and appraisal, inventory and awareness. I need to know that wherever *it* is, I am *here*.

After the most intense episode of his life, calling down fire on Mt. Carmel (see 1 Kings 18:16-40), the prophet Elijah fled for his life, battling fatigue, depression, and feelings of isolation as he lodged in a cave at Mount Horeb. There, God asked him (in 1 Kings 19:9), "What are you doing here?"

Knowing the answers to "How did I get here?" is the key to moving from here to there – not just geographically, but psychologically, spiritually, and emotionally. Have you ever taken a moment to ask yourself, "How did I get here?"

The problem is that if we've built "here" on fault lines, we can continue adding on and redecorating our "house," unaware that the ground is shifting beneath us. Then we feel the tremor, the beginning of the feeling that something is not quite right. Dissatisfaction is gnawing, disillusionment is hovering. When the stronger quake hits, we find that the elasticity of our soul has been stretched out and that the stability we've been leaning on in others is actually unstable. Resolve and resilience, the bounce-back, the comeback, and the "want to" all become wearied when we face these events. Like Elijah, we find ourselves at a place we don't know how to define. What we do know is that present conditions show us that we've built on fault lines.

Fresh paint and new carpet are not the answer. We need to determine if the damage from the shaking and quaking is permanent or if we can rebuild, reinforce, and restore.

Let's examine what a healthy soul looks like and how it can give us a framework for identifying the warning signs of a soul under siege.

CHAPTER 3
THE HEALTHY SOUL

We know the importance of understanding how you got to your "here," but what about moving from "here" to "there"? Can we expect to build correctly and move forward if we don't have a target or goal in mind? The healthy soul is our goal.

Our ability to enjoy our harvest and to reap in due season is, many times, commensurate with the health and prosperity of our soul – our emotions, mind, will, and heart. To the healthy, stable soul, ethics and values are congruent with the overall direction of one's life. These are the questions that guide decisions: What is good? What is honest? What is the responsible thing to do? What is the right thing to do?

Our interactions with others and the way we move through life should have an overarching, far-reaching, foundational ethic. When people ascribe to sound ethics and morals, we can count on them. We can trust them. And, for the most part, we can predict how they will respond to the circumstances and situations of life because they are people of principle.

Let's now take a practical look at what constitutes a healthy soul. People are considered mentally healthy if they are 1) in contact with reality, and 2) sufficiently free of anxiety so they are not significantly incapacitated functionally, socially, or biologically for any extended period of time.[2] Here are ten characteristics of mentally healthy people, which we could also refer to as signs of a healthy and prosperous soul.[3] We can then compare these to what an unhealthy soul looks and behaves like and the warning signs of a soul under siege.

1. *A healthy person exhibits the ability to function at full capacity both intellectually and emotionally.* Healthy people conduct themselves appropriately in a variety of contexts. The inability to keep a train of thought or form a coherent sentence could be signs of trouble, especially if these are accompanied by disproportionate emotional reactions.

2. *A healthy person reacts and responds to life's situations in a realistic and appropriate manner.* For example, a person with a healthy soul does not resort to destruction when angry or frustrated – he or she would not punch a hole in the wall during an argument or go through the house slamming doors and throwing pots and pans. Healthy people are able to acknowledge the circumstances of life without allowing those circumstances to dictate how they respond.

3. *A healthy person approaches life with self-confidence, optimism, and a sense of humor.* Healthy people have perspective and utilize mechanisms to respond with a positive outlook rather than becoming consumed by only the negative elements of

---

2 Paul D. Meier, MD, Frank B. Minirth, MD, and Frank B. Wichern, PhD. *Introduction to Psychology and Counseling: Christian Perspectives and Applications.* Baker Academic, Ada, Michigan, 1991.
3 Michael S. Pitts. *Living on the Edge: Spiritual Help for the Soul Under Attack.* Cornerstone Publications, Toledo, Ohio, 1994.

their lives. When people feel tormented, they can become pessimistic. They lose their ability to find humor or something positive in the situations they're facing and may even respond in anger or hostility to those who try to do so. They take everything too seriously.

4. *A healthy person has an unwavering sense of purpose in life.* Those who have experienced wholeness in Christ know that every day can bring an adventure in faith. They know that even when things seem to be going wrong, they will keep on living, firmly rooted and grounded in God's goodness and His ability to guide them to their next level and onward. A person who is losing the battle of daily life sometimes entertains thoughts of "ending it all" when the pain seems unbearable. We see this sometimes in the teenage years, when a bad break-up makes emotionally vulnerable young men or women want to end their lives because they can't see past the intense hurt, even when others try to offer encouragement and perspective. They have not embraced the greater purpose and bigger picture in their lives and can only see the trauma of their present situation.

5. *A healthy person relates well to a variety of people with the capacity for intimacy.* A healthy person accepts that others have different life experiences, national or racial origins, and economic conditions, and feels neither inferior nor superior to others because of them. A danger sign of a soul under attack is antisocial or reclusive behavior. Healthy people can enjoy being around others, whereas people struggling in the area of their soul often retreat from society and, in effect, drop out of life.

6. *A healthy person accepts the authority of legitimate people and institutions.* Healthy people understand the need for and benefit of identifiable leadership and are comfortable in their role relative to those people and positions. Rebellion is the product

of an unhealthy soul. Those who continually challenge the authority of parents, teachers, pastors, employers, and/or law enforcement officials are people who typically have deep-rooted emotional problems.

7. *A healthy person lives a balanced life and knows how to care for himself and others.* A healthy person functions in both dependent and independent roles. This shows that they have found a balance taking care of themselves and taking care of others. Self-centered people must always have things their way, while the other extreme imbalance is those who spend all their energy helping others until they themselves suffer physically, emotionally, and financially.

8. *A healthy person is dependable.* People who are in control of their lives have "self-authority." This means they are able to make a commitment, knowing their own abilities and limitations, and they consistently follow through on it. All of us know people who have a history of making commitments they don't keep. When a person is consistently late for work, church, social functions, etc., it is usually a sign that his or her life is out of order. When a person displays a pattern of being unable to fulfill obligations, promises, or commitments, there is likely an underlying soul issue.

9. *A healthy person is able to express and control strong emotions.* The healthy person is comfortable displaying strong emotions (whether positive or negative) in the proper context. Those with an unhealthy soul either repress or bury intense feelings or express them continually and without restraint. A person with a healthy soul, however, can experience extreme emotional situations without escalating or retreating.

10. *Healthy people are satisfied with their identity as God created*

them. Those who are healthy in their soul understand who they are and they are able to relate to others from a position of clarity and confidence. People who are unhealthy in their soul struggle with identity, with who they are at their core. This affects their relationships and how they engage socially.

WARNING SIGNS

Let me start by saying that I believe that life-quakes happen at precisely the times when we feel least equipped to deal with them. In fact, the feeling of running on empty brings us into that weakened state. My observation is that many people who experience such shakings have already been dealing with the erosion of negative emotions such as depression, grief, or despair for years.

As a society, we are losing our recovery time. The current speed at which life moves seems unrelenting, compounded by a 24-hour news cycle and social media, which keep us continually connected to the world. We carry in our pockets devices that expose us to the brutal and unfiltered events and opinions of the entire world at any given moment. Before we can process and move beyond one crisis or trauma, the next one is already here. In all of this, we risk the health of our souls. Our capacity is compromised. Our well-being is the casualty.

Abrupt Changes

The struggling soul who is in danger is the one who abruptly casts away a lifetime of proven principles and ethics. I have heard people say, "I no longer believe that," as they casually toss aside long-held beliefs. Of course, they conveniently find new belief systems that justify the abrupt changes, excuse their impulsive behavior, and allow them to walk away from responsibilities without feeling the slightest hesitation or remorse.

Years later, when the dust settles and time has done its work, people who have made these abrupt changes find themselves dealing with regret over the damage that has been done. They didn't have to quit their job and abandon their career so close to retirement, or they didn't have to walk away from their family to look for happiness somewhere or with someone else. But, when delusion is strong, people believe that their problems or stress are caused by external things, and so the faulty structures of their lives fall.

Shifting Ethics and Values

A person's set of ethics makes him or her predictable. To some extent, we can anticipate how ethical people will respond in a given situation. They can be counted on. Their responses are congruent with their guiding personal principles. Their actions and beliefs mirror each other. To them, convenience is not as important as conviction. It's not about what is easy, it's about what is right.

To the shaking, quaking soul, however, everything is subject to change. How it "feels," "what's good for me," or "what I want" become the mantra. Views that begin to dominate their thinking sound like, "I just have to do what's best for me," "I deserve more," or even, "God wants me to be happy." This is the language of those who are running from responsibility. They are signaling to the world that they are about to bail. In a clever and manipulative attempt not to be held accountable to ethical behavior, they simply shift positions as the quake begins.

Shared values are what hold a family, organization, church, or country together. Taste in music, restaurants, or vacation spots are on the periphery. We can debate about sports teams or social justice or the state of our nation, but in healthy relationships, we learn and are sharpened by these interactions. We grow from them.

If values move from "we" to "me," from "us" to "I," from mutual respect, responsibility, and load-sharing to "It's my time for me" and casting off established roles, relationships crumble. How difficult it is for people who have, for years, built with shared values to now find that the rulebook has been thrown out! They find that values are no longer shared and they are stuck being the responsible ones, picking up the pieces of a crumbling emotional edifice.

One of the toughest parts about trying to reach someone in this life crisis is that they pull away from those who care and seek out less demanding relationships that require less accountability.

When you find your ethics and values shifting, it is good to ask yourself whether or not your thoughts and behavior are honorable to who you have been and who you want to be. I think it is helpful in times of crisis to listen to your friends and the network of support you have in your life, and I mean really listen to them. Counsel only works if it has the capacity to help us change the story we're telling ourselves and others and the way we process painful days. It's helpful, in conversation with our trusted friends, to be able to have a dialogue. This is not to be misconstrued for arguing our point to win a debate, which alleviates us from hearing what others are saying. My point is that, if most of the people in your world are saying the same thing and you're saying something different, the way out of the crisis is to critically consider what you're saying and thinking and determine why it's so different from the other voices around you.

When we are in the midst of shaking, our foundation of ethics and principles sustains and helps steady us enough to get through. We keep going, keep doing the right thing, and we find that we are able to outlast the storm.

Radical Changes in Appearance and Dress

Over time, our personal style evolves. As we become adults, we typically land on what works for us and the environments in which we operate. From time to time, we update and upgrade. To the settled person, this is about taking care of our appearance and staying current. To the person caught in the rip tide of the life-quake, however, these changes have several important distinctions. They are:

Drastic – They simply want to make an external statement that they have become a different person. Some people shave off all their hair or start wearing extreme clothing styles you'd normally never see them in.

Not in step with their age or place in life – It's the classic picture of the clean-cut older guy who grows a ponytail, unbuttons his shirt, and buys gold chains and a sports car. It's the middle-aged mom who shops and parties with her teenage daughter after having been concerned about modesty only a few years prior.

Seductive/sensual in nature – Sometimes, people have makeovers. Some turn to gastric bypass after battling obesity. Some may have a nip here and a tuck there. The motivation seems different to me, though, when it moves from wanting to be your best, based on self-care and self-respect, and when it moves toward wanting to draw attention from others. Attempting to re-capture your youth or to experience things you think you missed out on can be a dangerous and slippery slope. It most often means something is shaking internally.

Reckless Spending and Suspicious Financial Shifts

A good indicator of a person's values is the way they treat money. As with the other changes, shifts from responsible and conservative patterns toward frivolous and carefree behavior signal that something is amiss. A connection exists between money and motive. Over-spending, over-leveraging, shady deals, secret spending, "get rich quick" schemes, and gambling with money you don't have are all red flags and warning signs of a soul out of balance. Opening a secret account your spouse doesn't even know about is highly problematic and cause for concern.

Something about money habits transcends basic accounting issues. Throughout the Bible, we see that money and the way it is handled reveal to us the character, nature, and direction of a person's life. Because our money issues are typically held privately, we should have at least one or two people who know of our financial moves and are trusted to hold us accountable and to question why we're doing what we're doing. Many times, when people don't include anyone else in important financial decisions, it's an indicator on a deeper level that they know the decision is wrong. Transparency, integrity, and honesty help us get out of a bad place or keep us from getting there in the first place.

Neglecting the Physical Factor

Mid-life brings what seems like an alien army of challenges to many of us. The aging process, stress, hormonal changes, and other contributors all seem to press in on us. When pressed, though, we tend to rise to the challenge, answering the call to manage and move forward. What we are not always aware of, though, is the toll this continual pressure takes on us physiologically. When pushed, our adrenaline kicks in, giving us the burst we need to face dramatic, life-changing situations and perform with abilities beyond our norm. Like a drag racer, we burn incredible amounts of fuel for a short, but glorious, burst of performance. But, when the fuel of adrenaline is gone, and the situation is still present, we turn to our reserves and begin to burn those, too. When this reserve is depleted and we have nothing more to pull from, we experience burnout.

Athletes who become injured are sometimes given shots of cortisone, a class of steroids that masks pain and reduces inflammation. The injury is still there, but they are able to continue playing without experiencing the full pain of it, and sometimes before they even know the full extent of the damage that's been done. In the same respect, we can think we are adequately managing hurt and pain for years, only to find out that when the mechanism we were using to manage it wears off, we are faced with the consequences of neglect and improper self-care.

This can be part of the life-quake – coming face-to-face with these extreme results of misplaced focus. Most people who have overcome the tumultuous season of mid-life can tell you that the physical changes, internal and external, cannot be ignored. Hormone levels fluctuate, metabolism shifts, and our physical well-being requires a new level of self-governance. Sometimes, truly, for the soul under stress, a bit of rest and a change in diet help restore balance when so many things can make us feel out of balance. This is why self-care is so critical – when our physical body is neglected, our soul is not far behind.

Emotional Extremes

Under normal circumstances, we all manage a certain level of uncertainty, unpredictability, and an ongoing list of stressors. When we are in a good place and healthy, it's amazing how much we are able to juggle at any given time. Ask any single mother about that one! Yet, when we are not at our best, and experience changes in the foundation of our lives, things we once handled easily begin to pile up, leading us to feel overwhelmed. We can feel like we don't know where to start to regain some semblance of order and normalcy or that too many things need to be done simultaneously. We think to ourselves, "I have so much to do that I do nothing." Of course, doing nothing compounds the feeling of failure, making us aware that we now have more to do because we've still done nothing!

Accompanying this is a lack of concentration. When people are overwhelmed and have a lack of interest, they may also find it difficult to concentrate. It can become an ongoing fight to keep one's thoughts on track. Tasks, responsibilities, and work that require prolonged attention range from being burdensome to impossible.

If those don't have your attention, think about this one: People in the grips of a life crisis often describe feeling numb, as though they are disconnected emotionally from their environment and the people around them. They feel as if they are seeing people and talking to people with whom they have no fundamental connection. Those experiencing the early shifts found along fault lines sometimes describe it like being in a fog.

I think this may be, in part, why we see such out of balance and dangerous behavior when people are experiencing these tremors. The rise of drug use, chasing illicit relationships, the vulnerability to affairs, the drastic changes in appearance, buying new sports car they cannot afford, etc., are many times a desperate attempt to *feel*. A person in this position is trying so hard to find something that reminds them what it feels like to be alive, to be loved, or to have the sensation they believe others are experiencing.

Changes in Social Patterns

Changes in social patterns are some of the most obvious signs of a life crisis. Individuals in crisis may withdraw from their existing social network – family, co-workers, or friends – in an effort to, as they see it, protect themselves or avoid addressing or discussing issues. They may become unwilling to participate in conversation or dialogue or avoid contact with others altogether.

Social media adds another layer of complication to these social issues and it can give us unique insight into people's social habits and patterns. Though it has certainly made it easier to connect with others across a multitude of platforms, for some, it also creates pressure to present the events of their day as highlights of a perfect life. Suddenly, we have a way to measure the approval of others. We find ourselves asking, "Did anyone 'like' my picture? How many people? Who was it?", "Did I use the best filter for my profile picture?", or "Did the 'right' people comment on my post?"

For people seeking attention, approval, or validation, social media can draw them in and create a reliance on these reactions as a measure of their self-worth. Those seeking isolation physically or socially can also find in social media a way to access the world around them without actually engaging in it.

One's behavior on social media can also be a cry for help. Posts and comments that once appeared to be healthy and contextually appropriate can often cross over into passive aggression, attention-seeking, or purposely vague content intended to get a response – posts about being "tired of drama," not being able to trust anyone, or outright attacks on others can all signal a soul in distress.

When we experience a life-quake, we desperately want to fill the void left by the damage, and social media offers us an easily accessible vehicle for revealing any and every detail of our lives, for venting our full frustration, or for hiding behind the mask of a highlight reel that is anything but real. Used in this way, it creates an artificial environment that cannot provide the solace our souls are seeking.

People who exhibit these unhealthy social patterns have lost sight of the confidence and fulfillment that can only be found through a relationship with God and a knowledge of our identity in Him. They may be unaware or unwilling to acknowledge that they have slipped into these unhealthy patterns, however, and must begin by honestly confronting them. This is where we see the benefit of supportive relationships that bring a stabilizing force to our lives – whether it is family, friends, mentors, or counselors. They can see our blind spots, hold us accountable to the ways we've said we are committed to live, or provide godly counsel and encouragement.

Others are able to recalibrate by taking a break from social media altogether, using the time away to sharpen their focus and re-evaluate their motivation and priorities. A fresh perspective helps us walk in gratitude and move away from the self-centeredness and self-pity that can trigger these patterns.

Abandoning Passions/Interests

Individuals going through difficulties often stop doing the very things they once loved and enjoyed. These things no longer bring them pleasure when they are experiencing stress or crisis. Abandoning a prized garden, award-winning athletic pursuits, or artistic endeavors, or even giving up simple hobbies that have always been a part of their lives are noticeable negative behavioral changes. People describe being out to eat with familiar friends only to find themselves feeling terribly bored and wondering when they can go back home. There seems to be nothing that brings fulfillment or a sense of purpose. In short, everything feels like a chore. It feels like a chore to take care of ordinary family responsibilities and it feels like a chore to move through life at a healthy pace.

When we are experiencing this or any of the other warning signs, we often seek escape mechanisms. A new and healthy habit or hobby could bring needed freshness and stability into a person's life. It's never too late to try something that's good for the soul – maybe a book club or painting class or volunteering in a local community-based organization. It should be something that is consistent, organized, and upstanding. Otherwise, our negative feelings and behaviors will lead us to unorganized, unhelpful, and unhealthy events and gatherings that place us in further emotional, psychological, and/or physical danger.

A Faith Crisis

Most of my time and my counsel are within the context of Christianity. Not exclusively, but by far the largest portion of my time is spent helping believers be better at believing.

Along the way, I've discovered an unintended consequence to believing and behaving within the framework of the Christian ethic. When believers are overwhelmed and find themselves in an existential crisis, they can begin to question beliefs that had at one time been firmly settled.

We must be careful not to cannibalize our own faith. It's amazing how easily we turn on ourselves! We suppress our feelings because we are depressed in our emotions. Rather than "faithing" it, we start faking it. We condemn ourselves for being human and then we feel bad about feeling bad! It seems as if we cease to be on our own side. When people live in a continual state of being at odds with themselves, having no resolution, and always feeling as if they are coming up short, many find it easier just to give up.

The problem with the way Christianity is presented and taught to us many times is that it makes us acutely aware of our weaknesses. This erroneous thinking can produce a sin-consciousness. Somehow, by becoming a Christian, we now keep track of our sins – a burden we didn't even have when we were sinners! We have become indoctrinated to identify more with what Adam did to us than with what Christ has done for me! Rather than rejoicing in a righteousness that is given, not earned, and an acceptance of grace, we somehow fault ourselves for our humanity that, for as long as we live, we will never be delivered from.

To the soul in the midst of struggle, knowledge becomes a burden. We may feel like we now know enough Scripture about joy to know that we shouldn't be upset or depressed. We feel as if we know the proper scriptural answer to all the questions we're facing. The struggling soul, like Adam, hides from God, avoiding prayer and a spiritual environment, which produces yet another level of guilt and condemnation.

This allows self-doubt to enter into the equation. I find that what most people feel as doubt expressed toward God is nothing more than self-doubt. People become disappointed in themselves, ashamed of the feelings or the temptations they're experiencing, and they begin to wonder where the strong believer is who once tackled problems and wrestled them to the ground with their faith. Now, they are not so sure they have what it takes anymore.

Sometimes, people express anger toward God for not delivering them, for allowing things to happen, or for plans that did not work out. This is why I say it has to be self-doubt, because even if you are angry at God, it is the indication that you know He's there. You cannot be angry at a nothing.

Let me turn a corner here and encourage you that God is big enough to handle our frustration and anger. There's a whole book in the Bible called Lamentations, where Jeremiah told God, in essence, "You have prevailed over me, You are bigger, You are stronger, and ever since I started working for You, I've had nothing but trouble" (see Jeremiah 20:7). In the Psalms, David bemoaned the number of enemies that troubled him, the prosperity of the wicked, and how those who troubled him increased. In 2 Corinthians 12:8, Paul prayed for the thorn in his flesh to be taken away. On and on it goes. I hope it doesn't offend your religious sensibilities to remind you that Jesus, in Matthew 26:39, tried to negotiate His way out of the cross at the beginning of the prayer at the garden of Gethsemane – of course, He did ultimately submit His will to the will of the Father.

This is what I believe is the key for this faith crisis:

Real relationships have to have conflict resolution and our relationship with our heavenly Father is no different. Nothing gets settled by avoidance and silence. Even when our prayers lack the eloquence of the Song of Solomon or our favorite grandparent's beautiful articulation, I believe God would still rather hear our honest hurt and frustration, rather than coming to the garden and asking us the question, "Adam, where are you?"

CHAPTER 4
THE SUPERMAN SYNDROME

What causes us to move from healthy to unhealthy behaviors? What erodes the confidence and clarity we once seemed to possess, that helped us build stability and consistency into our lives? I believe it has much to do with what I call the Superman Syndrome. We feel like we have to be the superhero of our own story, yet it can cause us to hide our true, flawed selves behind the hero's mask. We want people to believe we are stronger than we really are, that we don't need to be rescued, and that we can defeat any foe who challenges us. But, what happens when the pressure to be perfect becomes too much to bear?

My wife, Kathi, and I have two grown children – a girl and a boy, in that order. When our son was four years old, Kathi gave him a pair of zip-up Superman pajamas, complete with a red Velcro cape. He felt completely empowered by these pajamas, especially the cape! While wearing it, he was totally in character. He *was* Superman. He "flew" through the house, scaled furniture, dove onto beds – you get the picture. He became so fascinated by it that eventually he refused to take it off! Except for the occasional bath, he *had* to have it on. I believe he may have even worn it to church a time or two.

The world loves Superman. I mean, we *really* love Superman. Since his first appearance in Action Comic #1 in 1938, his brand has gone global. His famous "S" logo is instantly recognizable the world over. It's even one of the most popular tattoos for men! His debut in the comics made that issue the most valuable comic book of all time. In 2014, a copy sold for $3.2 million![4] Everyone loves Superman, and who can blame us? He's stronger than a locomotive, he can leap tall buildings in a single bound, he has x-ray vision – oh, and he's bullet-proof.

His alter-ego, Clark Kent, is not so glamorous. Somewhat nerdy, somewhat clumsy, he is just an average guy – perhaps even a bit below average. The two personas are one person, however, and both are rendered powerless by kryptonite, a rock from Superman's home planet Krypton.

Here's my point: Everyone loves Superman, but not even Superman is Superman all the time! How many of us try to shed our inner Clark Kent for the glory of being Superman all the time? We are convinced we can sustain our superhero status, but can we? I am challenging you to take the cape off, come out of the phone booth, and introduce the world to the other you – the real you. The one who isn't as strong as people think. The one whose vision is not always perfect. The one who doesn't talk about it much, but who is continually aware of and avoiding his or her own kryptonite.

Sometimes high-level leaders experience low-level things.

---

4 Sheridan, Patrick M. "Original Superman Comic Sells for Record $3.2 million." CNN Money. http://money.cnn.com/2014/08/25/news/companies/comic-record/index.html (accessed January 31, 2018).

When people fear that others will find out that they are not always performing at the level they project, they tend to isolate themselves and become image-driven rather than relationship-driven. One key that healthy people have in common is long-term friends they meet with frequently, allowing valuable conversations to emerge from these relationships. These are not people they are in charge of or people who work for them, but simply friends on a peer level with whom they are able to be open and sincere.

I have seen others, who didn't have those long-term quality relationships, crash and burn. Isolation and being image-driven caused them not to open up or to reveal the times when they were struggling. Somewhere, they needed to ask themselves why they were more afraid of building honest relationships or of others finding out they're a human being who has human experiences? Why be more afraid of these things than of crashing and burning?

All people have the potential to fail. All will experience temptation. All people will have seasons when they're not at their best. You are not excluded from the term "all people." Being surrounded by people who know you and with whom you can be open helps us to navigate the many seasons and situations of life.

The Cape Escape

Maria had become someone different. She was no longer recognizable to the people who had known her for years. Her appearance and fashion had changed significantly, but the biggest change had already happened internally. The friends and relatives she had known for years were unable to figure out her formerly firm, now floating, ethics and values.

Previously, they would have used such words as "stable," "consistent," and "dutiful mother" to describe her, but there had been a shift. It didn't happen in one day. In reality, she had been drifting little by little for some time. Wearied with the routine and responsibilities of life, marriage, and parenting, and burdened by the pressure to flawlessly manage it all, she decided it was "her time." "I'm doing what's good for me," she would say.

Her clothes became a bit more revealing and her disposition a bit more flirtatious. Family events were put on hold while she and her group of girlfriends went out – these friends were younger, single, and had fewer responsibilities, and she envied them. She had been feeling like her life was passing her by. She had become bored with her old "mom friends" and defended the actions of her younger, free-thinking friends. She now condoned the very behavior she had taught her children was wrong.

Her husband gave her space, reasoning that it was just a season she was going through. By the time they got around to serious conversations, she was deeply entrenched in her own life-quake. She blurted out that she loved him, but was no longer "in love" with him. She didn't want to live like this anymore. She wanted out! Family and friends pleaded with her, but it was too late. The children were devastated, her parents and in-laws were shocked, and her husband was ashamed.

She quickly cut off every dissenting voice and started her new life, leaving broken hearts and broken dreams in her wake. She flaunted her new-found freedom on social media, posting photos with her younger and hipper crowd, complete with younger, cooler guys.

Little did she know that years later, she would find herself longing for the very things from which she had walked away. It would take years to repair the damage and nothing was ever quite the same.

Where Have All the Heroes Gone?

One of the toughest things about life is the loss of innocence. What do we do when our heroes fall? However misplaced our favorable assessment of our heroes may be, we cling to it until, inevitably, we find that ones who became our personal Superman, are really Clark Kent. The cumulative disappointment of seeing the flawed humanity of the people we look to, whether civic leaders, church leaders, sports figures, or family members, leaves us with a sense that there are no more heroes. This disillusionment is no better than the illusion that brought it on.

At some point in life, all of us will experience the crushing feeling that one of our heroes is gone – and probably more than once. This kind of life-quake can be difficult to navigate. Some people can shrug it off and get down the road without much of a glitch in their step, while others lose their bearing and fall into cynicism and a "what's the use" mentality.

Sometimes, we face the harsh realization that our focus on the superheroes caused us to overlook solid, stable, unsung heroes all around us. Could it be that we have mislabeled the people who count and the people who do not? For people who have neglected normal, long-term relationships only to be infatuated with the position and prestige of others, the cold reality, like the person taken on a money scam, is that perhaps our own greed, neediness, or insecurity made us susceptible to it.

CHAPTER 5
HOPE FOR THE SOUL

We've covered much of what constitutes a life-quake and how we create the conditions for one in our lives, so let's turn a corner now and look at another way we encounter unexpected issues and the hope for recovery built into the equation by a God Who cares for us.

One of the parables Jesus taught that I think best illustrates this subject matter is found in Matthew 13. When you read this parable, you find Jesus talking about a farmer who sowed good seed in his field, but an enemy sowed tares in the same field while this farmer slept. The man was unaware that tares had been sown in his field until the wheat started coming up. It starts "good" – with good seed in the man's own field. It ends "good" – with gathering the wheat to the barn at the time of harvest. It starts good and ends good, but it's messy in the middle. And, remember, the middle is where we find so much potential for shifts and shaking.

I don't care what you're involved with, the middle is messy. Marriages start off with good seeds and good plans, but then they get messy in the middle. People in mid-life commonly experience crisis before eventually, hopefully, leveling out. Let's face it – the middle of anything reveals how we've been building.

Here is why I think there is hope for the soul. The man was asleep when the seeds were sown. Everyone gets tired! Did we actually expect that because the man owned the field, he should never rest or get tired? Let me say it again: Everyone gets tired.

Being asleep is analogous to being unconscious to something. Many of the tares sown into our soul were put there when we were unaware of it. An enemy has done this, not you.

This is interesting because this was somewhat of a common practice at that time. If you really wanted to mess up your enemy, you waited until he was asleep and sowed things in his field that he wouldn't want so you could mess up his harvest. The parable continues that, right when his harvest was starting to come up, the tares came up with it. And his servants asked, "Where did these tares come from?"

Note that the man did not become aware of the tares until the wheat began to come up. It is possible for seeds to lay dormant until you begin to spring up! Many times, your greatest battles are just before your biggest breakthroughs. Have you ever felt like asking why the things you are dealing with in your life are surfacing now? You were unaware that something else was also in your field. As you were trying to make strides forward, the tares appeared. Or have you ever noticed that while you've got your faith moving toward your breakthrough, things start coming up in you and you say, "Where did that come from?" You didn't even know that was in you! You thought that was over, because you sowed good seed into a good field, and you're a good person, doing all the right things. Right?

Sometimes, though, the arrival of tares is the indication that wheat is growing. The undesirable things that are coming up indicate that you're coming up, too! The enemy sowed things in you when you were tired, hurt, unsteady, or battling – God didn't do it, the enemy did! Sometimes, it's sown in you and you're asleep to it. You're unaware of the fact that while you were growing up, someone sowed something into you and it never showed up until you decided to do something for God.

The servants in this parable asked where the tares came from because they knew the farmer was a good man who sowed good seed. They wanted to know if they should go and pull up the tares. The man said, "No, let them grow together until the time of the harvest." You have to know that God cares, otherwise you'll think this farmer is "care"-less, or operating without care. You'll want those tares to be gone and pulled up. He said to let them grow together until the time of the harvest. Otherwise, if you start pulling up tares, you're going to damage the roots of the wheat.

One of the problems we see from this story is that the people trying to pull things up are not reapers. The man is saying that when the harvest comes, he'll tell the reapers (see verse 30). This implies that the ones asking are not permitted to pull anything up! Be careful with people who can see something in you that they're not qualified to deal with. You can't just let anybody walk through your field and start pulling stuff up!

What I love about what God is showing us is that the man trusted the good seed he had sown. God knows the strength of the seed He's put in you! He's not worried about those tares.

The tares have no power over the wheat! I know you feel like they do, because you weren't expecting them, or because the ground shifted suddenly, but God knows the strength of the seed He's sown in you and He trusts it!

When you feel the pressure and you see the tares, remind yourself that God trusts what He put in you. According to Philippians 1:6, He who began a good work in you shall perfect it! Your harvest is not seasonal, it's revelational! As soon as you understand what's going on in your life, as soon as you get this issue settled, you can step into your answer.

The hope for the soul is found in trusting that the wheat is greater than the tare, and in knowing that there is a harvest season coming for the good that has been sown.

Let's go back to the idea of the middle – this middle where we find ourselves susceptible to shifts and shaking. Joel 2:17 says, "Let the priests, and the ministers of the LORD, weep between the porch and the altar." That's the middle. We need the ministry of others because so many people are dealing with the middle. Between the outer court and the most holy place, somewhere in that middle, we need some "priests" to weep and to say, "Spare these people…" Otherwise, according to this passage, they'll say amongst the people, "Where is their God?" The idea there was that they didn't want the non-believers to think they didn't have a God or that He didn't care. Verse 18 says that the LORD would be jealous for His land and pity His people, answering and saying, "Behold, I will send you corn, wine, and oil, and you shall be satisfied therewith and I will no more make you a reproach among the heathen." Continuing, verse 21 contains the encouragement, "Fear not, O land, but be glad and rejoice for the LORD will do great things."

That's the point I want to make to you! God cares for you! There is seed sown in your land, so fear not, for the LORD will do great things. The story in Joel 2 continues with a description of how things will end with good. It's just messy in the middle because the enemy has tried to sow bad things in your field. You have to keep your mind on the end, on how this thing is going to wrap up. According to 2 Corinthians 1:20, all the promises of God are yes and amen!

The passage in Joel 2 ends with the familiar promise in verse 25 that God will restore the years that have been consumed and destroyed. The enemy may have sabotaged you, and maybe you can even identify areas where you yourself planted carelessly or dangerously, but God is able to redeem you! He is a restorer!

The God Who Cares

Not only is the seed we've planted good seed, but the God who watches over it is good, too. He's invested in us in profound and personal ways. One of those is the way He cares for us. He's so good at protecting us that, half the time, we may not even realize we're being protected.

Every so often, though, we get clued in to the fact that God is doing something around us, for us, and with us. He cares for us His way, teaching us throughout the process. He's not afraid to lean in on us – even if we say we don't want to talk about something! We need to have this revelation that He cares for us because it's not always going to feel like that's what is happening. It can feel like He's fighting with us – cutting our flesh, crowding us, etc. But, it's all part of Him caring for us.

The fact that God would be referred to as "your God," or be called the God of any man, is in itself a unique concept.

Generally, the biblical picture is that the greater possesses the lesser. But, God has allowed Himself to be possessed by us. He is my God. I love that because there is a dual possession going on here – though He possesses me, He allows me to possess Him. Rather than just making me the object, He also puts me in a cooperation process with Him. I am His, but He is also mine.

God has an investment in us that He is determined to get out of us. This is what you have to know going into life and your relationship with Him. God knows things you don't about yourself and He knows your full potential. He alone knows what He put in you and of what you're capable. He says, "For Me to get that out of you, I've got to get you out of one state of thinking into another state of thinking, and I can't do that always when I'm catering to your comfortability. I have to push in on you a little bit and I've got to move a few things around, so just go into it knowing that I am your God and I care for you."

Let's go deeper into this concept of how God cares for us. One of the things God shows us is the ability to discern difference. It's part of wisdom. Light is different than darkness. Land is different than sea. Birds are different than fish. Man is different than woman. You have to understand difference because you can't get to harvest with sameness.

You can't know yourself by yourself. God has to put us together, in our families, in our churches, in our communities, and around people who are different. It may not feel like it, but God puts people different than you in your life because He cares for you. He can't put another YOU next to you!

If you don't understand difference, you will treat your

friends like enemies. That's a terrible and foolish thing. Or, you'll give your enemies access to places in your life only your friends should have. You don't know who to listen to if you don't understand the power of difference.

God tells us that certain things are different – different in measure, levels of glory, capacity, mantles, callings, etc. But, He also teaches us the power of things that are "same" or "like." When God is trying to teach us things we have never known before, He uses things we are familiar with, that are like what He's trying to teach us. This gives us a reference point. We don't have to be around a righteous man for Him to teach us about one, because He tells us that a righteous man is like a tree planted by the rivers of living water (see Psalm 1). You may have never been around a righteous man, but God can teach you by telling you what one is like. And, you can draw information from what a tree planted by a river is like – stable, deeply rooted, growing – and understand something about a righteous man. God also shows us that an unrighteous man is not like a tree; he's different. An unrighteous man is like grass that comes up fast and is quickly cut off. If we understand what is "like" and what is "different," we can be better prepared for all God wants to teach us as He cares for us.

Another way God teaches us is geographically, by where we find ourselves. In the absence of a book of promises, the Old Covenant people had a land of promises. Where they were physically and geographically spoke to them about their walk with God. So, when they were in drought, that meant they needed to consider where they were, because He said that if they walked with Him, He would send rain to their land in its season. If their land did not produce harvest, they needed to ask why.

So, they walked through the land, building altars, digging wells, and naming places based on what they had learned about God's care along their journey. The principle was that generations would come behind them and they should not leave a geographical place until they understood the revelation of why it was given a particular name.

It's hard to be in a place in life that you're trying to get out of or away from, and God says, "You're not leaving this place until you understand how you got here. And I know you're mad, sad, or frustrated, but remember...I care for you." He cares for us, even in a hard place, a dry place, or a place that seems to keep shaking.

I have found that our willingness and ability to hear are often in direct proportion to the discomfort of our situation. You can come to a place that makes you really, really ready to hear. You'll wake up in the morning, certain that everything is a sign from God because of how badly you need to hear from Him! You'll be looking for a word in songs on the radio, in conversations with your kids, or maybe you'll walk outside, see a squirrel, and take it as confirmation from God that you're not nuts! When you're ready to hear, I believe a word is already on its way!

Power and Parables

A parable is like an adapter that you put between the power source and the thing you're using so it can handle the power. The adapter allows you to take the power without destroying the thing you're trying to use. God has truth for us that we're not fully ready for, and we can't handle it full-strength, so He wraps it in parables. The great thing about parables is that you think you get them at first, and the more you think about them, the more you keep getting from them! It keeps unfolding in such a way that you're not getting too much at one time. God cares for us, and if He gives us a truth before we're ready to receive it, it will harm us. But, if He withholds it from the people who are ready, it will harm them. That's why it's wrapped up in a parable!

Jesus used parables because He knew He was talking to people at many different levels every time He taught, so it became a matter of, "He who has an ear, let him hear." Those who are ready will get it and those who aren't will just hear a nice little story. He does this foundationally by describing His words as seed and our hearts as soil, telling us that there's nothing wrong with the seed, and that our harvest is based on our ability to carry the seed He gives us.

Our capacity to hear determines the depth of what we receive. Atmosphere determines the ability for a seed to penetrate. Jesus creates the atmosphere for us to hear, having explained to His disciples that the ability to understand parables has been given. We are not the "them" who had ears but wouldn't hear. We must have ears to hear. It's the key to understanding how God cares for us and how to successfully navigate uncertain seasons.

CHAPTER 6
EXPERIENCING A QUAKE

After an earthquake, we don't stop living. We get up, dig in, and rebuild. We reinforce what was weak and emerge stronger than before. We recover and restore.

Mexico City experienced an earthquake on September 19, 2017 that measured 7.1 on the Richter scale. More than 200 people were killed and thousands were injured.[5] Tens of thousands of structures, including buildings, schools, shopping centers, apartment complexes, and houses were damaged or destroyed.

In the weeks following this massive earthquake, I was able to have a conversation with Pastor Ofir Pena, the leader of our Cornerstone Global Network of churches throughout Mexico. By this time, it had become obvious that many people in the city were living in a state of fear. People were not sleeping well and were experiencing high levels of tension. In fact, they were

---

5 Nicole Chavez, et al. "Central Mexico Earthquake Kills more than 200, Topples Buildings." CNN.com. http://www.cnn.com/2017/09/19/americas/mexico-earthquake/index.html (accessed September 27. 2017).

probably living with elements of post-traumatic stress disorder. They were living with an unnerving sense of vulnerability and no longer felt safe. They seemed to feel that life was beyond their control. Fear and anxiety were palpable and pervasive.

Some of the structural casualties were luxury apartment complexes that had cost developers somewhere around 2 million pesos. These were fancy, high-end apartments. It was only after they were destroyed in the earthquake that it became clear that these units looked impressive on the outside but had not been built properly on the inside.

These things trigger several parallels with the life-quake:

•After something is destroyed, do we rebuild? And how? What if the damage is too severe?

•Who do we trust to help us rebuild? Were they part of the initial disaster? How do we know they are qualified now?

•What if we feel like we are damaged beyond repair?

In a literal sense, if the complexes were destroyed and then rebuilt, we have to ask if we would even want to move back in, knowing their structural flaws had been exposed and they were prone to collapse! These flashy new buildings created quite a stir, but now we know they were not up to code. Everyone wanted to move in then, but what about now?

As we all know, people, too, can be superficial. We can probably all think of those who are looking for long-term relationships but are still measuring by short-term ideals, building on the fault line of searching for someone who is attractive, but not stable. Let me tell you, stability should be attractive to you!

When people are in relationships, they should be asking themselves and the other party (rather than just looking at curtains and furniture), "What is the quality of decisions over the history of your life? Who are the important voices you value? (Truly, you're only marrying the voices they see as valuable and worth listening to.) What is their normal daily routine? Spending habits? Views on money? Moving into relationships like a person moves into an apartment, never having asked more than superficial questions, is risky. Flashy looks nice, and everyone wants to move into it, but it's ultimately unstable. No matter how you decorate the apartment, it doesn't change what it's made of!

We also see that the closer we are to the epicenter of a quake, the more damage is done. While quakes are common across Mexico, this one was unique because its epicenter was so close to Mexico City. If this earthquake had been any stronger, at that proximity, the entire city could have been leveled. I have found that the closer people are to the epicenter of a life-quake, the more damage they sustain. The closer the relationships are, the closer in proximity to those who are shaking, the greater the damage.

Pastor Ofir noted that, on the Sunday following the earthquake, nearly every church he knew of was filled to overflowing. This stands out to me because it is similar to what we saw in the days following the September 11, 2001, bombing in the United States. On the Sunday after that attack, churches experienced a surge in attendance – the largest attendance in recent history![6] When we feel vulnerable, fearful, and we are experiencing a quake, we want to turn toward God and allow our faith to help us recover.

6 Gerald L. Zelizer. "Quick Dose of 9-11 Religion Soothes, Doesn't Change." USA Today. http://usatoday30.usatoday.com/news/comment/2002/01/08/ncguest2.htm (accessed September 27, 2017).

Authorized Inspectors

Inspections are performed to ensure that a certain quality and standard is being met so what's being built can endure. Building a life that can withstand the shaking and quaking means making provision for proper inspection.

Inspection is uncomfortable, unpleasant, maybe even embarrassing; it requires that we expose ourselves and what we've been building. It is laborious and it slows down the building process; everything has to come to a halt to allow the structure to be thoroughly investigated according to code. We may not like the process of inspection, but it comes down to the fact that no one should have more invested in the safety of the structures of your life than you. Inspection is necessary to ensure integrity.

So, who is authorized to do the inspection of the life you're building? God never intended for us to do life alone, carrying the weight all by ourselves. We all need a support network of peers and overseers that will provide stability and safety. We cannot solve long-term problems with short-term people. We all should have people in our lives who modify our behavior, people we act differently around – not because we're faking it, but because there's a respect factor and being in their presence calls us higher. When that relationship is understood, we acknowledge that it is not a peer relationship that requires approval to inspect – oversight does not need permission to crowd us. We don't have to be ready for the conversation. We need someone who can come up to us without permission and note, "You don't seem like yourself. What's going on with you?" It's part of the pattern we find in the way God cares for us.

When we see that corners are cut, inspections are rushed,

or that those entrusted with the process don't do their jobs, the entire structure of our lives collapses. I have seen people over the years who become addicted to counseling, to telling their story over and over. However, a proper support network will help you deconstruct that story, see the God-factor in it, and walk with you toward measurable goals.

When the quakes of life come, your "building inspectors" assess the depth of your foundation, the strength of your supporting mechanisms, and the integrity of your covering. They know your goals and the blueprint you're working with, they check in with you during the process, and they hold you accountable for what you've committed to building.

We need to be mature enough to submit to the insight of others we've allowed into our building. Don't expect to build strong structures if you're going to bail on someone when you don't like what they say to you! We all know those who are experiencing a shift or a shaking who turn to isolation and inward retreat rather than allowing others to have access to them. Inspection exposes what we're trying to build, but it ultimately strengthens us.

For those who are experiencing quakes, for those who have been building on fault lines, and for those who are witnessing others in the middle of trouble, I believe there is power to recover and to end up better than before.

Processing Pain

The truth is that everyone has pain; no one is exempt from it. Even a successful life is not without pain. When the shaking and quaking hit, however, we can easily get jolted by the impact or trapped in the rubble of crumbling structures. But, the issue is how we process this pain. There are healthy ways and unhealthy ways.

We must start with identifying our pain and the negative emotions attached to it. Knowing yourself and knowing your wounds is the beginning of self-care. Someone else may trigger it, but the wound is still yours to care for. Self-care asks, "What can I do about this?" It asks, "Where does this fit in with who I am and who I hope to be?" You may never feel like you've fully recovered, and that process is different for everyone, but knowing the starting point is the only way to measure progress.

The benefit of self-care and paying attention to one's own wellness is that it liberates us from feeling as if we have to wait on someone else to help us. While we've already covered the importance of a support system, it is possible to find yourself in a place where the people around you care deeply for you but may lack the skills to help you. In those times, we should attempt to assess our own well-being and give attention to the areas of our lives that are causing concern.

The added blessing of pursuing and understanding our own wellness is that it affords us the opportunity to see signs and patterns in others who may be struggling, giving us a chance to be a help to them, as well. Many people in our sphere of relationships will face times when everything is shaking, and if we are conscious and aware, we can be for them what we may not have had for ourselves. We who saw our own need for authorized inspectors and reinforced support systems can progress to seeing that need in others. This is how we move from personal restoration to being equipped to help others through the process.

In the next section, I want to take you deeper into this concept of caring for others.

CHAPTER 7
STAND IN THE GAP

The hardest test to pass is the one you don't know you're taking. When people are in the middle of a life-quake and attempting to restore and rebuild, one of the greatest assets they can possess is a stable, loving, and spiritually mature friend. The aftershocks of a major shift can cause separation and isolation, hindering the journey towards peace and restoration. The presence of such a friend or colleague plays a pivotal role in rebuilding.

It matters how friends and loved ones analyze the aftermath of a life-quake. Seeing and processing the pain and failures of others requires humility, sensitivity, and maturity. When God allows you to see the sins and mistakes of others, up close and personal, you must understand that it is possible that you are being put to the test – one you may not realize you are taking! The question then becomes: "Can I be trusted with someone else's trouble?" The objective here is to properly assess the present while simultaneously operating in faith to see the future.

It is impossible to fill one gap with another gap. I know that sounds like a simplistic statement, but you have no idea how many times I have witnessed this phenomenon. You can see it unfold in the everyday lives of people at work, at school, or at home. It won't help the struggling soul if you don't know how to properly handle their trouble.

"Live creatively, friends. If someone falls into sin, forgivingly restore
him, saving your critical comments for yourself. You might be needing
forgiveness before the day is out. Stoop down and reach out to those
who are oppressed, share their burdens and so complete Christ's Law.
If you think you are too good for that, you are bitterly deceived."
Galatians 6:1-3 (MSG)

To emphasize this point, let me direct your attention to how it is phrased in the King James version: "…ye which are spiritual, restore such an one in the spirit of meekness; considering yourself, lest thou also be tempted."

All relationships have a reciprocal element. Whether positive or negative, it is impossible for two people to interact without both being affected. True spirituality requires the ability to bring ourselves to another's position or perspective to accurately identify and relate. This action opens up the unseen world of connection, where transfers of information and energy move back and forth between the two. We need to respect and understand this potential because of the transformative possibilities, both positive and negative. This is how we start to fill gaps and reinforce sound structures correctly, with sure foundations of knowledge and wisdom.

God has called us to this kind of authentic spirituality. It is bold. It is persistent, but also patient. It is an act of faith with underlying spiritual principles that cannot be ignored. It does not allow us to be indifferent to or to rejoice over, even for a moment, the demise of another.

Every military operation requires highly skilled medical units. What soldier would go into battle knowing there was no medical team assigned to him? Professional sports teams spend huge amounts of money and rely heavily on a myriad of expert trainers, doctors, and injury treatments. You cannot sustain a winning team while neglecting players' health. Similarly, civil organizations and governing bodies of every kind have made detailed preparations for emergency management. Countless lives are saved every year because of the safety and security systems that have been put in place. Experience teaches us that a well-organized disaster plan can mitigate the potential trauma of tragic events.

Staying in this context, when courageous soldiers are wounded in battle, we reward them with a medal of honor. But, does the Body of Christ do that for our own warriors? When athletes are injured and leave the playing field, we cheer and applaud them to voice our encouragement. Does the Body of Christ? When civil servants are harmed in their workplace, they are awarded compensation and restitution. Do we do that in the Body of Christ?

The Body of Christ, the Church, should not only have the same mentality when it comes to their injured or fallen, but *we* should be the model for the world at large. We should be "the city built upon a hill" that Jesus spoke about in his Sermon on the Mount, and "the light of the world" (see Matthew 5:14). As followers of Christ, we should be the most prepared for casualties, having the foresight and fortitude for complete restoration.

Spiritual warfare is now a well-accepted phenomenon in most church cultures. But, it still shocks me that we are somehow surprised when someone falls, messes up, or gets out of line. I think much of the initial negative reaction is out of disappointment and a feeling of being let down. It's our own unpreparedness, though, that really is the issue. If you prepare for something, you will move into action faster and adapt to each situation as it necessitates. You've already said, "This is going to happen. It's not what we want, but it's part of the landscape we live in, so let's be good stewards of the resources we have at our disposal." Be spiritual!

Our lofty expectations of fellow believers are a trap. The Bible calls it a "snare." It really is just a fault line appearing in our own lives, which distorts the truth about the rich grace under which we should be living. In the absence of grace there is only one result – "religiosity," or what is commonly known as a religious spirit. Just a simple head-turn from a religious person, wielding that monstrous log in their eye, can take out a whole crowd of well-meaning church folks in a matter of moments! I believe the military term for this is "friendly fire."

FAITH IS A CONTACT SPORT.

We must understand and acknowledge that we are in a fight – and there will be casualties. To embrace the example set by Christ and live a faith-orientated life in a spiritual dimension, we must expect to attend to injured and disenfranchised people. We have to become both a people and a culture of restoration. It is not only a necessity for our survival, but it is a critical element of our highest calling – to reflect and represent the core teachings of Christ, the highest Lawmaker and Authority of our belief system.

Rules of engagement must be established, of course. We should not be justifying sinful behavior or an incongruent lifestyle. We certainly don't want those on our team playing from a different playbook, promoting what is contrary to our core ethos or values. Setting examples for our children, adolescents, and those outside the church family is so important. Building bridges of trust rooted in character, high standards, and commitment to godliness will bridge the gaps of both generation and mission.

Gaps exist in the uneven places, the shaky places, and the vulnerable places, so the spiritual among us must be equipped with a "seek to restore" mindset, making visible to all of God's people the mysterious operation of His Spirit as we cooperate, under His direction.

When someone is drowning, pointing out the NO SWIMMING sign can wait.

Our being saved and transformed involves others. It is not based on some individual merit system, completed in isolation. When Christ taught us to pray, He began with the clear statement of "Our Father" (see Luke 11:2). We are intrinsically and inextricably connected, and that's how God has designed it to work. Your ability to live a fully blessed life must involve getting down and dirty in the imperfect lives of others. Our collective faith, at the end of the day, says, "It is His goodness, not ours, moving in and through us, that comes to the rescue." He is faithful at lifting us all up and out of troubled waters. He is faith not just at saving us, but at repairing and restoring us, as well – and always with the potential of reaching a higher level.

"Who art thou that judgest another man's servant? To his own master he standeth or falleth. Yea, he shall be holden up: for God is able to make him stand."
Romans 14:4

THERE WILL ALWAYS BE A GAP BETWEEN WHAT WE ASPIRE TO BE AND WHERE WE CURRENTLY FIND OURSELVES.

This concept above is what I call the fault line between position and condition. Part of the Christian culture should be, "If you see a gap, stand in it!"

Every believer has the potential to be a bridge of restoration. Imagine what our churches would look and feel like if this was a serious goal. When gaps are filled, then "those who used to serve God" would not be part of our lexicon or vocabulary. Our churches would be filled to overflowing, I have no doubt.

Multitudes have been wounded and fallen by the wayside – too many to even track or count. If we would just care for the people God has entrusted to us, we could be in a continual state of revival. Revival should be a normal state for the church, not an event or a method of evangelism.

You can go through a season of prolonged attack and start acting outside of your belief system. How many people within our collective scope used to serve God, were raised in someone's church, or were baptized when they were younger, and have lived a whole other life since then? They used to have a relationship with God, and then something happened. Maybe someone close to them died, and they couldn't figure out why that happened. Maybe they fell amongst thieves.

Maybe they got tired of dealing with Pharisees. Who knows what happened to make them fall away? Sinners don't expect Christians to be perfect, but what they don't like is when we make them feel like they are the only ones struggling or the only ones who have had a rough season. They're watching how we treat our own. When we treat our own badly, they ask why they would even want to join up to us when the person beside us for years was cast away.

The Path for Prodigals

Our God is the God of the never-ending chance, not just a second, third, or fourth chance. So, there is always a path for the prodigal. If our sons and daughters are going to come home, we must have a place prepared for them. This place is called restoration. We must learn from the errors of our past and become people who will recognize the gaps when they appear and stand in them.

What are some of the things we see in the life of the prodigal?

• He was wrong (impulsiveness, impatience, and ambition clouded his judgment)

• He disrespected his loving father

• He got what he wanted and left

• He had a season of riotous living

• He joined himself with the wrong crowd

• He didn't see the famine coming

• He hit absolute bottom

•He finally came to his senses

•He remembered his home

•He decided to go back home

This a complex story, but one I think many of us can relate to at some level. Here is my objective in looking at this well-known piece of Scripture: The father was always ready and prepared to receive his son home.

The son knew the way home. His life-quake had nearly destroyed him. He had built unwisely on a fault line and fell through a gap of his own doing. The only safe place he ever knew was back in his father's house, where even the servants lived well and at peace. If we are willing and prepared, the Father will draw his prodigal sons and daughters home.

I AM AGAINST THE ASSASSINATION OF PRODIGALS

What do I mean by this? The father's celebration when the prodigal returned shows that his heart was not punitive, but redemptive. The father set the tone for the environment in which he wanted his son to be received. The whole household and the older brother were to take their cues from the perspective of the father's heart. To be clear, there are times when restoration involves a process and measurable progress, giving us the framework for receiving prodigals. Ultimately, though, prodigals will become champions of recognizing gaps and standing in them if we handle the restorative sequence the correct way.

This concept is further exemplified in the account of Jesus washing the disciples' feet in John 13. After the Last Supper, Jesus took a basin of water and a cloth and began to wash their feet. Peter saw this humble act of service as beneath Jesus, perhaps reasoning that they should be washing His feet, which would seem more spiritually appropriate. The statement Jesus was making was, "If I don't wash you, you can have no part of Me." At this point, Simon Peter yielded. Jesus continued, "You don't know what I'm doing now, but you will understand it later," adding, "All of you are clean, except one."

Jesus' aim was Judas. Judas needed to be cleansed. So, rather than singling him out, embarrassing him, or pointing out his sin, Jesus simply included everyone else. This is the true heart of restoration, Jesus-style.

> *"If I then, your Lord and Master, have washed your feet;*
> *ye also ought to wash one another's feet. For I have given you*
> *an example, that ye should do as I have done to you."*
> *John 13:14-15*

So much of our ministry of restoration is not public, on the platform, or even publicized by others close to the situation. The example of Jesus is always the best.

IT TAKES MORE COURAGE TO STAND IN THE GAP OF RECONCILIATION THAN IT DOES TO FAN THE FLAMES OF DIVISION.

Is it just me, or does it seem like the whole world is seemingly about to come off its hinges? The spirit of division and separation is resting like a thick cloud over so many people, polluting the environment of unity like I've never witnessed before. We're constantly being separated into categories, like products on a grocery store shelf. Left or Right, Red or Blue, Black or White, Citizen or Immigrant, Wall or Bridge. I could go on and on with these paradigms that pit nation against nation, community against community, and neighbor against neighbor.

Even our Christian communities, who read the same Bible, are seemingly intent on perpetual contention, focusing on the things that separate us. The things we disagree on are now central. It is difficult to find the places of unity being celebrated in the Body of Christ. People, by and large, I believe, have lost their ability to reason a matter out. Their biases and leanings have become strongholds and open debates. Common courtesies are absent. We are starting to refuse as a society to celebrate sensible, thoughtful, and intellectual dialogue and those who wish to promote it. Calm discourse is not popular, and this is especially evident in our media and their current affairs programming.

One of the obstacles we face in pursuing reconciliation is quite clear: social media. Well, let's name it for what it has become: anti-social media. The rise of hostility and divisiveness on these platforms is breathtaking. It has proven how ugly people can be when they can hide behind a profile, a like, a hashtag, or a re-tweet. I believe God's people are being put to the test. My real concern, though, is that I think we are failing.

We are giving all the attention to the bombastic, the verbal grenade throwers, the instigators, the crude, and those who fuel the fire of division. Where is the platform for the peacemakers? The people who will stand in the gaps and bring reconciliation – where are their voices? It is a moral failure to allow those who cause division and strife to be the loudest voices in our society.

It seems to me that the voice of the Church should deal with the condition of our hearts. Irrespective of what side of an issue we find ourselves on, our hearts should never be hard. We also are called at some level to be the conscience of our society. We should not be afraid to address controversial issues, and we certainly should not be confined to the corner in silence. We cannot feed on a steady diet of division and discord. This renders us incapable of building the internal fortitude we need for unity and restoration.

Reconciliation protects our rights. In its purest form, it always allows for diversity and difference, so our individuality is not obliterated. Personal autonomy and freedoms must exist in the process of reconciliation so that we are not robbed of our expression and opinion. There is what I call a "mystery of power" – this meshing of the individual and the collective. If we truly embrace it, we will ascend to a level of authentic unity that will have revolutionary results. We must avoid the temptation of always having to be right in every situation. We must root up the thorny weeds of selfishness and pursue reconciliation at every level.

Let me tie this all together under the context of fault lines and the cracks that I see appearing in both the social and cultural networks. With all of this energy focused on a few hotbed issues and their viral nature, the seismic activity of this divisiveness is like a ticking bomb. Distrust is shaking our communities and it is gathering momentum.

It is time for us to address our issues, certainly, and they are serious. But, we must come together, shrinking our gaps, not widening them with hateful rhetoric. I truly believe we must start the reconciliation process now! The trajectory we are on is unsustainable and my heart is heavy by what I am witnessing.

May we speak the heart of God and move the heart of man on these issues of injustice, such as racism, poverty and the poor, the unborn, human trafficking, modern slavery, and more. The list could go on and on.

I believe the world is waiting on us. There is great power in reconciliation. We have access to supernatural gifts and the wisdom and counsel of the Spirit to find a way to address the gaps of injustice for the greater good of the human family. There is a way to create an environment for good to win, for people to rise, and for those who have fallen to get up again.

> *"Every kingdom divided against itself is brought to desolation; and every city or house divided against itself shall not stand."*
> Matthew 12:25

This division is a "weapon formed against us." My faith says "it shall not prosper" against God's people, but we must be proactive at every level of our relationships, whether personal or corporate, to close the gaps.

CHAPTER 8
THE PATH BACK HOME

I would like to get into some of the previous chapters' ideas a little deeper. In my life, I really want my efforts to count. My goal here is to promote the keys for us to start to fill gaps with permanency. The lasting effects of our work will be based upon the materials we use. Spiritual principles produce spiritual results.

We can create things, move things from the immaterial into the material, if we stay focused on the tools that God has given us. With love as our motivator and guide, we can achieve the seemingly impossible.

Reconciliation

I outlined some of the imperatives of reconciliation previously, but I want to go a little deeper here. Jesus was sent to the earth because there was a gap. His assignment? To fill that ever-widening distance between God and man. This moment in history was a time not dissimilar to what is being experienced globally today. Division and schisms of every variety existed in the understanding and the expression of faith towards God.

So, what was God's first step? Reconciliation! Through this radical act of love, God was clearly communicating His intention for change, through an intervention of reconciliation. He was showing us a new way, a better way – one that brings freedom, empowering all people with the potential to live in a spirit of unity.

"For God so loved the world that He gave." We know John 3:16 so well, but let's look more closely. Reconciliation always begins with an act of unconditional, sacrificial love from one party. This is our model for standing in and bridging gaps.

Reconciliation is difficult if our carnal nature is dominant. It requires a deeply spiritual attitude to create the conditions for forward motion. The latency and stationary aspect of a breach can be intimidating, to say the least. Sometimes the fiercest battle is fought in the very beginning – just to see any progress may require some heavy lifting in the spirit realm. God counted the cost for us, though, making Himself the author of our reconciliation.

> *"But, don't begin until you count the cost. For who would begin*
> *construction of a building without first calculating the cost*
> *to see if there is enough money to finish it?"*
> *Luke 14:28*

As ambassadors of Christ, we must understand the first step involves some act of reconciliation in the spirit of love. The principle is clear. Once people are reconciled to God, they are called to be reconciled to others. This is the replication effect that Kingdom principles embody. It is sequential in operation and always brings us into alignment with His ways, which is really His will. Our prayer is always "On earth, as it is in heaven."

The need for reconciliation must be bigger and more important than any personal or group agenda. God has called us to be agents of healing and deliverance and personal agendas undermine our efforts in this process. We shouldn't move away from our foundational truths in controversial situations, but we must always be ready to respond. As gaps appear, we stand in them.

As we stare failure, hate, pain, and all kinds of injustice directly in the face, it is vital that we don't revert into an "us versus them" mentality. Reconciliation is always an "our" situation. This is how we ensure an authentic operation of the ministry of reconciliation. If there is a gap, it is approached as *our* gap. We pray "*Our* Father in heaven," not "My Father in heaven, excluding all others who don't measure up."

The mature believer understands the power of the altar, the place of laying things down, to become a better steward of the things God has entrusted to us, especially other souls. We live in a hostile world, a world of strong opinions that I believe have become our modern idols. To be truly effective in reconciling, we must place our opinions on the altar or we will fail the test before we even begin.

Your need to be right, heard, or validated will disqualify you from the ministry of reconciliation. A spiritual person understands the humility and selflessness required to be a reconciler. This spiritual act is a reward in itself. It unlocks spiritual power for insight and knowledge and promotes new avenues for forward movement. As Jesus promised in Matthew 5:5, "The meek shall inherit the earth."

God saves the individual, but His plan is always for that soul to be part of a community, God's family. The concept of family and community is a cornerstone of our faith. I currently see it under attack from every angle. We must be fully aware that we live and operate in a world governed mostly by a secular, nihilistic worldview.

I see it unfolding. We are dehumanizing each other and reducing our "neighbors" to mere objects and ideologies. We don't see the person first, but only what they represent or believe (or post on social media!). We are losing our sense of human connection, so easily disregarding each other, preferring isolation and comfortable bubbles, and letting our insecurities run rampant. We must understand that gaps are widening in the present climate and have the potential to create havoc for the next and future generations. If we do not act as peacemakers, those who follow us will not be able to rise.

When we distance ourselves, we tend to demonize those who disagree with us. A hallmark of maturity is holding differing opinions and still being able to stay in a relationship. The further I am from you, the easier it is for me to disregard you, to invalidate your total existence. I'm sure we've all heard people make the proclamation that someone is "dead to me."

Jesus spoke to this very issue. His assignment, I believe, was to stand in the breach between God and man, so that men could then stand in those breaches for one other. Through this act of reconciliation, we now have the power to do it for each other. "Love God and love your neighbor, as yourself." Jesus stated that this simple commandment (see Matthew 22), aligns with and fulfills every law that governs relationship.

It takes more courage to stand in a gap than it does to sow seeds of division. It takes more grace to discern the goodness and potential in another person than to see their faults or failures.

WE MUST BE ABLE TO STAND IN GAPS WITHOUT BECOMING THE PRESSURE THAT WIDENS THEM

The world is watching. So is God, I believe. Will we become the "called out ones" that He has instructed His church to be?

What does it mean for us to be fully reconciled? I believe the actualization is the act of reconciling another. You were reconciled to God, not to just punch your ticket into eternity with Him. You were reconciled to become a reconciler.

Restoration

Restoration has to do with the action of returning something to a former owner, place, or condition. As with reconciliation, it begins with an *action* – an act of returning. Something is coming back, full circle. I will address this concept, the bounce-back, in more detail in the next chapter.

So, for the context of this chapter, I want to keep driving the point of what an important role spirituality plays. Many times, when gaps appear in people's lives, our actions, although sincere, can come across as punitive. Restoration must not carry an underlying sense of punishment or condemnation. We have to shift restoration from a carnal state into a higher realm. The carnal mind is at enmity with God. It's hostile to God. It does not subject itself to the laws of God.

We need an awakening – perhaps, really, a re-awakening. We need a fresh move of the heart and mind into the Jesus-style of restoring people. All people in all times sin, fail, make poor decisions, and are ensnared in varying stages of life. The consequences of our wrong-doings cover a wide gamut of outcomes. Those who have been entrusted with the care of others, whether we be friends, counselors, or church leaders, are the stewards of the well-being of others. We are not called to do for others what they can do for themselves, but to do on their behalf what they cannot do for themselves.

In every walk of life, people are judged and held accountable, many times, for the worst episodes of their lives. How will they escape from self-imposed prisons if those who are called by the name of the Lord don't help set captives free?

God did not send his Son into the world to condemn it, but to restore it. "Do unto others as you would have them do unto you" (see Luke 6:31) is the familiar exhortation. His ways are not our ways, especially when it comes to the treatment of those who are in need of spiritual restoration. All of us at some point have made a mistake and received some form of punishment because of it. It's not a good feeling. There are obviously levels of mistakes and levels of punishment. The secular justice system is all about trying to fit crime with punishment. Let me be clear. The Church does not exist to execute criminal justice. If egregious crimes have been committed and someone is proven guilty, then there are laws that govern that. As a civilized society, we have all agreed to do it this way. There are protocols. It's not perfect, far from it. It's a secular system, but we are called to simultaneously operate in a different system, a higher system.

The people of God and their leadership, I believe, are at a crossroads in time and direction. We have such an opportunity before us to truly reflect as a people and a culture what the love of God really looks like, especially how we deal with those in our own family and community. Does it get any clearer, simpler, or more fundamental?

*"A new commandment I give unto you, That ye love one another;
as I have loved you, that ye also love one another. By this shall all men
know that ye are my disciples, if ye have love one to another."*
John 13:34-35

LOVE IS CENTRAL TO EVERYTHING
SPIRITUAL – GOD IS LOVE.

Restoration without love at the center is just a punitive, restrictive, chained-and-bound, guilt-and-shame, ordeal.

Let's look at some of the things I gleaned off the dictionary definition of restoration.[7] We need tangibles and guideposts. Restorers, take note.

1. Returning to a former owner

   •Restoration begins with a return to God. This should be the foremost intention of the restorer. Restoring is repairing a person's relationship with God and themselves.

   •People stumble and lose their way because they shut off their divine source and supply. We need to help them return to their spiritual home.

   •Outward actions and reactions are just signs of an inward condition.

   •God looks at the heart (ours, too!), and so should we.

   •The miracle of restoration occurs in a spiritual dimension.

---

7 English Oxford Living Dictionaries. Oxford University Press. https:// en.oxforddictionaries.com/definition/restoration (accessed January 31, 2018).

2. Returning to a former place

•One of the keys to spiritual power, is the power of place. The physical aspect of place is providing a person a safe, stable, and friendly environment. Make it practical, make it familiar, and offer solutions.

•Church, fellowship, prayer, worship, and the presence of God are all place-related aspects of restoration.

•Never underestimate the power of a familiar place. Returning to a place where a person has had a deep spiritual experience can be powerful during the process.

•Identify spiritual markers that exist in people's lives. Those can be important milestones to help them find a way back home.

•The personal aspect of place is important to the restorative process. Repairing and rebuilding a soul is a complex process. The re-instatement of self-worth, self-respect, self-love, and self-confidence (trust) are invaluable. These are truly the "places" of personal restoration. [*I cover this concept of the power of place more in-depth in a message series entitled* The Mystery of Power *— see* Resources page.]

3. Returning to a former/proper condition

•Things break down. Things wear out. Things get messy. Science calls it entropy. Things left to themselves bend toward chaos. It requires exercising a positive force to return things to a former condition and to order.

•Life has innate power and energy. It is always in

motion and moving in any given direction. When things are moving away from center, due to being unattended, it is good to first slow things down.

•Our lives, with all their dynamic energy, always have the potential for collision, accidents, and collateral damage. Repair and restoration should be part of the plan.

•Most products have the name of the manufacturer or creator on them. This name tells you where you need to take it when it breaks down. You can't take a Rolex to a Timex store, and you can't take your Mercedes to a Ford dealer. It matter where and to whom you take something when it is broken.

•Restoration should not be cyclical, but transformative. It should be forward moving, always on a higher trajectory and seeking new levels. God wants us not just to recover, but to flourish.

•True restoration includes the potential to be included back into circles of trust.

Intercession

Intercession is standing in the gap. It is going to God on someone else's behalf. It is acknowledging that, on this journey called life, there will be times that people do not have the strength or faith they need for themselves and they will need an intercessor.

Intercession requires spiritual strength and commitment. It becomes an act associated with a priestly position. There is usually a great spiritual and emotional bond between the intercessor and one for whom they are interceding. Even if separated by distance, time, or lacking personal contact, this spiritual connection fuels the intensity of the prayers. We cannot watch the enemy just pick people off while they are isolated and alone – we must be sensitive to when the Spirit of God is calling us to intercede for others.

Numbers 16:47 details Aaron's actions as a plague swept through the Israelites' camp following Korah's rebellion. It states that Aaron did as Moses commanded and ran into the midst of the congregation, making atonement for the people. He stood between the living and the dead and the plague afflicting them was stopped. This is a picture of standing in the gap. It is our calling and responsibility to go to God on behalf of others.

The people God wants to lift out and draw to Himself often may not look like they even need help. Trouble can be quite deceptive in its early stages, but can eventually become a plague. If we understand the true spirit of intercession, God will trust us with those who are in trouble – knowing we won't look down our noses at them or judge them harshly.

The Levitical Model

The name Levi means to "join" or "accompany." The children of Israel had built a golden calf as an idol of worship while Moses was on Mount Sinai (see Exodus 32). When asked who was on the LORD's side, the tribe of Levi made a statement in joining themselves to Moses. Out of the bloodline of Levi, God called the Levitical priesthood. There was something in them that caused them to stand out and stand strong. The Levitical priesthood gives us a framework for understanding intercession.

The Levites were associated with the glory. Their role was vertical and horizontal – vertical, in the sense that they held the glory and sacred things in high regard, and horizontal, in that they bridged the gap and closed the space that existed between God and his people. Their portion and inheritance wasn't land like the other tribes were given. Instead, God gave them charge over places called cities of refuge. There were three on the east side of the Jordan and three on the west side of the Jordan. A city of refuge was a place of protection from the "avenger of blood," who was authorized to pursue a fugitive.

These cities were strategically located so that it never took anyone more than one day to get there. The idea was that if you needed to get to one, you could get to them quickly. If the avenger of blood found you outside a city of refuge, he had a legal right to kill you. People would flee to these cities, and the Levites were responsible for protecting the people who were fleeing.

The Levites had to build bridges over ravines, rivers, ditches – wherever there was a physical obstacle. The goal was to get the fleeing person to a place of refuge as quickly as possible. They could not just build a walkway or a pathway; it had to be something greater. This wasn't some hiking trail that one needed a map and compass to find. It needed to be a highway – a higher way!

A regular part of the Levites' function was to clear this highway of stumbling blocks and obstacles and to ensure that the way was clearly marked. Whenever someone came to an intersection or a crossroad, the direction for the city of refuge was marked clearly so they didn't have to stop running to read it. In the same way, intercession leads the way, clears the way, and shows the way.

The city of refuge was a unique place – the gates were never locked. Cities of that time were always fortified with guards and locked gates, but these gates were never allowed to be locked, so that no matter when someone showed up, the gates could be opened. It was illegal for anyone to pursue fugitives once they were inside the gates. And, it was not only for the children of Israel. The cities of refuge were for them *and* for strangers – they were for everyone.

These cities were well-stocked with food and water because the Levites were required to take care of fugitives when they arrived. This is a picture to us that parallels the imperative that there should be "meat" in the house of God (see Malachi 3:10). Those who are thirsty can be satisfied. We cannot wait to stock up until a bunch of people show up. We have to prepare now!

The Church is supposed to be this city of refuge! We're supposed to have the strength to stand as the Levitical priesthood in our time, determined that the avenger of blood will not take people from us. The enemy was hunting us down, but Jesus bought us back! He had the wherewithal to do it and did it willingly. He chose to be our kin, to be related to us. He's our city of refuge and our kinsman redeemer.

May God give us a heart and an anointing to reconcile, restore, and intercede! May we be a city of refuge, a place of safety from the avenger of blood, and a safe harbor from stormy seas.

CHAPTER 9
BOUNCE BACK BETTER

We know that we won't get through life without taking some hits. We also now understand that it is our duty to stand in the gap for others who have been wounded. So, now I want to address how we, and those we are entrusted with, can continually make progress no matter what obstacles we have faced or are facing.

I believe one of the major keys is resiliency – the power to bounce back. It is one of the greatest capacities you can develop. There is a human power to it, but there's also an anointing to do it that's bigger than just turning over a new leaf. It's bigger than making a resolution. There is a power that comes from God that will cause you to bounce back when everyone else says you can't and when it feels like everything around you is shifting and unstable. Even when you have made the wrong move or decision and your faults are exposed, God can still cause you to bounce back!

Genesis 49:19 details the story of Jacob blessing his sons at the end of his life. He said about Gad, "A troop shall overcome him, but he shall overcome at the last." The expanded meaning of Gad is "his reward shall come at the end." Gad is a picture of the bounce-back anointing. There will be a season where he is overcome, but the promise is that he will overcome at the end. I believe if you tap into this anointing, it doesn't matter what has happened, you can bounce back better.

I like the words of the prophet Micah: "Rejoice not over me, my enemy, when I have fallen, for I will rise again" (Micah 7:8). You may remember, back in 1974, the Rumble in the Jungle – it was Muhammad Ali versus George Foreman. I remember it because it was when Ali introduced the "rope-a-dope." For eight rounds, Ali was being hit and looked worn down and beaten. Everyone wondered what was going on with him. But, in the 8th round, it all changed. He bounced back and won this now historical boxing match. [8]

Or, maybe you watched the 2017 Super Bowl when the New England Patriots overcame the largest deficit in history, securing an overtime win over the Atlanta Falcons. The sports network ESPN recorded that the Falcons had a 99% probability of winning 20 different times during the game.[9] The Patriots scored 31 unanswered points in the last 18 minutes – it was really something extraordinary. Without making enemies of any sports fans reading this, that was an incredible example of the concept, "It ain't over till it's over!"

---

8 Robert Cassidy. "Rumble in the Jungle: Muhammad Ali vs. George Foreman." Newsday. https://www.newsday.com/sports/boxing/muhammad-al-vs-george-foreman-rumble-in-the-jungle-on-oct-30-1974-1.11873736 (accessed September 27, 2017).

9 Jordan Heck. "Super Bowl 51: 10 Incredible Stats from Patriots "Win Over Falcons." Sporting News. https://www.sportingnews.com/nfl/news/super-bowl-51-2017-score-mvp-highlights-stats/1q2ya5azlbi5y162wakk9gv96v (accessed September 27, 2017).

You may have struggled for a season, or made some bad choices, or done things that made others turn away from you, but God can still cause you to bounce back. Failure is never permanent unless you quit. We all fail, but if we keep moving, keep walking, keep swinging, keep believing, keep praising, keep praying, keep standing – if we don't give up, we will win. Even if all you have left is God, you still have enough to start over again!

IF YOU ARE GOING THROUGH HELL DON'T STOP

I attended a boxing match recently and noticed several things during the match and behind the scenes.

Everyone has to learn how to take a punch. It has to be built into the structure of your life. When you give your life to Jesus, you have to understand that faith is a contact sport. You have an adversary and the world is not set up for your success. You can't fall down the first time you don't get your way. You can't give up too easily.

In one of the matches before the marquee match, a boxer got hit below the belt. Not only do we have to learn how to take a punch, but we also have to learn how to survive a low blow. Have you ever had someone do something to you that was just low? It's hard to register when people smile in your face and stab you in the back, or when you find out that the very person grinning at you was working for your demise. You're either going to quit or come back stronger.

Because of where I was sitting, I was able to see what was going on in the corner of the ring. I got to see a few different styles of teams. I noticed that one fighter's team was very professional. Everyone knew their role and responsibility. Every time their fighter got tangled up, he would look straight over to his trainer, who would then give him a signal. Thousands of people were screaming, but he just fixed his eyes on his trainer. At one point, someone else on the team shouted to him, "Throw a left hook!" That person was sat down immediately by the trainer!

It made me think of this principle: If you're going to rebound, it matters who's in your corner. It's hard to have a bounce-back with an unprofessional team. It is incredibly important who you listen to in critical moments in your life. The noise in the arena of life can be deafening and disorientating, but you have to stay focused on the right voice. That sideline "expert" yelling advice from the 25th row is more interested in his hot dog and soda than your well-being – he's not thinking about your success and your future!

Another match began with a new fighter and team – it was evident to me that, compared to the first team I was watching, nobody knew what to do or what role they were filling. The fighter was good, but I said to myself after the first break, "He's going to lose this fight." Not because he wasn't talented or brave, but because his team was so disorganized! At one point, I counted at least seven different people yelling instructions to him. Seven. They didn't even seem like helpful instructions, either. "Knock him out!" and "Hit him harder!" were what I heard. They were getting louder than his trainer. It was total amateur hour, and the guy with the gloves on was taking all the punches. Then, the guys in the corner got into a fight among themselves!

Does this sound like any situations you have been in? The trainer only has about a minute between rounds to give clear and coherent advice and take expert care of cuts and swelling, so it's crucial that everyone is on the same page. During this match, though, the trainer actually turned at one point and asked me, "What round are we in??" I couldn't help myself, so I yelled, "We? You aren't in a round, but your guy is in the 10th round!" It was really only the 3rd round of the fight, but the boxer looked like he was in was in the 10th round, all because of who was in his corner.

If you're going to bounce back, you're going to need some people in your corner who know the right signals to send you, who can keep you from getting distracted, and who can call out to you, "You can do this! You can win this thing!" The guy who won had one voice among the crowd, one guy who knew the right signals to send, who could keep him focused. It didn't matter what the crowd was shouting or what anyone else was saying, he only had to look to one person when he found himself in a clench, to get the signal for where he needed to go. The other guy looked over when he was tied up and he was trying to find one voice out of the noise from the seven.

If you're going to be resilient, you have to learn who to ignore. Some people in the crowd are for you, but they can't help you! During one match, a very enthusiastic fan came up out of his seat and was yelling at the boxer. He was this loud guy in the 18th row, eating nachos. He was a fan and a supporter, but nothing he had to say could help the fighter. Find the right team, people who are really in your corner, and don't get caught up with folks in the crowd! These other people can't really help you, and some even want you to fail. They are the same people who are predicting your demise, making lots of noise. At the end of the day, none of them go home with you and live your life. Take command of your life and use wisdom for the team you want in your corner.

The secular world understands the importance of resiliency and it is frequently emphasized by its leaders. Dean Becker, the president and CEO of Adaptive Learning Systems said, "More than education, more than experience, more than training, a person's level of resilience will determine who succeeds and who fails. That's true in the cancer ward, it's true in the Olympics, it's true in the boardroom."[10] And, it's true in life. If you develop the capacity to bounce back, then you are going to succeed in life.

I remember hearing an interview with NFL running back Walter Payton – he was asked why he immediately jumped up after getting knocked down. He replied that he had to make sure that whoever hit him knew they didn't hurt him. That's deep right there. When you take a hit, it's not time to stay home from church and hide for three weeks. What you ought to do is jump right up and to let the enemy know that he may have hit you, but he didn't hurt you! Walter Payton carried the ball 3,838 times,[11] running the equivalent of nine miles, getting knocked down every five yards. He's in the Hall of Fame because he bounced back 3,838 times. If you get hit, jump up, and get back in the game!

It is said that under pressure, we don't rise to the occasion or even our expectations. Instead, we fall to the level of our training. In the moment of pressure, you don't have time to feel good or to look for someone to clap for you; you have to remember your training. You've been trained in prayer, you've been trained to stand and to walk, and the good news is you

---

10 Diane Coutu. "How Resilience Works." Harvard Business Review. https://hbr.org/2002/05/how-resil
11 Frank Litsky. "Walter Payton, Extraordinary Running Back for Chicago Bears, Dies at 45." The New York Times. https://www.nytimes.com/1999/11/02/sports/walter-payton-extraordinary-running-back-for-chicago-bears-dies-at-45.html (accessed September 27, 2017).

don't have to feel good to do it. You can keep going while you're scared, when you're hurt, or when you don't feel good. That's what an overcomer looks like. That's what victory feels like.

Before the attacks on September 11, 2001, the financial services firm Morgan Stanley made sure their people were fully prepared for what to do in case of catastrophe. They may not seem like a target, but they were the largest tenant in the World Trade Center at that time. They had 2,700 employees working in the South Tower on 22 floors. When the first plane hit the tower at 8:46 A.M., Morgan Stanley started evacuating employees *one* minute later. All told, the company lost only six employees, despite receiving an almost direct hit.[12] Why? Because at the moment of attack, they went back to their training. This is what we have to do, too. We have to know who's walking with us and who we're supposed to listen to when the crisis hits.

GOD'S PLAN IS ALWAYS FOR YOUR COMEBACK TO BE GREATER THAN YOUR SETBACK

Look at this familiar story from the life of David. In 1 Samuel 30, David returns to Ziklag to find the city torched to the ground by the Amalekites. All the wives and children had been taken captive. David and his men lifted up their voices until they had no more power to weep. It's okay to cry – there is a time for everything. But, there is a moment when you've cried long enough. David was greatly distressed – the people spoke of stoning him because of the grief in their own souls. It was a terrible scene, but what did David do in the midst of his pain? He encouraged himself in the LORD his God.

---

12 Michael Grunwald. "A Tower of Courage: On September 11, Rick Rescorla Died as He Lived: Like a Hero." Washington Post. http://www.washingtonpost.com/wp-dyn/articles/A56956-2001Ocy26.html (accessed February 3, 2018).

There will be times when you will have to be your own cheering section. Look yourself in the mirror and declare: "God is with me and for me. His hand is on me, and He's been good to me." Sometimes, you have to say it when you're facing a stack of bills or feeling sick in your body or when it seems like nothing good is going on around you. Clap for yourself! Declare that God is on your side and that the Lord Himself will fight for you. If you don't have anyone to encourage you, learn to encourage yourself. Learn how to thank God for your own breakthrough and your own open door. Praise God until something begins to happen for you!

Your confession of faith must be that the future you is going to outdo the present you. Further in the story of 1 Samuel 30, David asked the LORD, "Shall I pursue after this troop? Shall I overtake?" The LORD answered, "Pursue, for you shall surely overtake them, and without fail, you shall recover all."

Remember that the pronouncement over Gad was, "A troop shall overcome, but he shall overcome at the last." Gad ended up establishing a specific area and the people who dwelled there became known as the Gadarenes. Many years later, in Mark 5, Jesus came out of the boat to this same place. There was a man there who was dealing with a troop – a legion of demons had overtaken him. He was overcome, but what he didn't know was that he was in a place with a prophetic promise. Jesus asked him, in verse 9, "What is your name?", and he answered, "We are legion, for we are many." Jesus opened up His mouth and with one word brought deliverance and freedom to this man – this man who had been thrown in the fire and in the water, this man who had his dwelling in the tombs, this man no one else could help, this man there was no hope for, this man they had all said was out of his mind. This man was now clothed and sitting in his right mind when the people of the city came to see him. This man is a picture of you – bouncing back by the words of Jesus.

People are going to be amazed at you. They're going to say, "The last time I saw you, you were rock bottom and bitter. What has happened to you?" And, you're going to testify, "Yes, that's very true, a troop had overtaken me, but I bounced back and I bounced back better!"

When it felt like your life was thrown into chaos, you could've lost your mind and no one would've faulted you for it. You could've said, "It's too much," and no one would have disagreed. You can have a setback where you lose your momentum and your rhythm, or you get bad news that knocks the wind out of you, or you go through a tragedy, or have unanswered prayer or a financial crisis. But, God wants to give you a bounce-back. You may feel like you're in the ring, but Jesus has always been in your corner!

Sports Illustrated, some years ago, made a list of the greatest bounce-backs and comebacks, ending their list with the #1 comeback of all time – Jesus' resurrection after His crucifixion.13 After all those sports moments and historical events, they wrote that the greatest comeback was Jesus getting up out of the grave.

This ability to bounce back is part of your DNA. It's part of your spiritual heritage. It's inside of you. You come from a lineage and a history of people who walk out of fiery furnaces, who survive being thrown into lion's dens, who walk on water, move mountains, and pray and praise their way out of locked prison doors. I wish I could promise you that after getting saved you'll just have bluebirds chirping over your head and

---

13 "Bouncing Back Big-Time." Sports Illustrated, Vol. 95, No. 19, November 12, 2001 (accessed February 3, 2018).

you'll hear angels singing God's praises everywhere you go, but the truth is, you won't get through life without having your foundation tested.

The enemy wants to wear you out until you quit – if you get worn out and quit, you'll give up hope. But, hope is built on the promise that if you don't quit, you can't lose! Your reward is not always evident in the middle, but it's evident at the end. If you withstand the shaking and keep walking, you will get to your reward. No matter what is going on, determine that you will not give up.

The Self-Imposed Setback

Have you ever had to bounce back from something you did to yourself? Have you felt the ground shaking beneath you, knowing that you cut corners and built carelessly? You wanted it to be the devil, but it wasn't. Most people do well when facing the attacks of the enemy because they know we have an adversary and they know that, when we get pushed on, we'll push back. But, we aren't always good at bouncing back from the things we do to ourselves.

Something can get into Christian theology that gives us the faith to bounce back from something that happened to us, but, somehow, we feel like we deserve it if we did it to ourselves. But, that's the whole problem. You don't get what you deserve! If you got what you deserved, it wouldn't be grace!

It's hard to have a bounce-back when you feel like you can't get out of it because you created it and you feel like you deserve it. Some people don't get healed because they don't take care of their bodies and think they don't deserve healing. I'm not giving you an excuse to live foolishly or not to take care of your body, but I am telling you, there are people who limit themselves and believe that they cannot go to God for healing. Taking care of yourself, which we all should do, certainly, is not a prerequisite for healing. In fact, in some instances, not taking care of yourself might be why you need healing in the first place!

Let's go a little deeper and talk about two triggers of a self-imposed setback: shame and self-sabotage. When people are bound by shame, they have the internal feeling that they are uniquely broken and cannot be fixed. They feel like there is something deeply wrong with them. If traced back through life, you will find that shame has a voice and it usually repeats a similar sentence in different contexts.

"You're not supposed to be here." It began when a parent first said it to you. It opened you up to rejection issues. Throughout life, in social settings, relationships, or a new job, the voice always tells you that you're not supposed to be here. You feel out of place and misplaced.

"You will always be taken advantage of." Shame has a good memory and will help you keep track of all the negative events of your life – the times you were lied on, ripped off, or betrayed run together in an unbroken chain, in a story you tell yourself, forgetting all the good things that have also happened along the way.

Shame has a voice, but the truth is that you are not uniquely broken, but similarly broken, as many others are. You can be repaired, and you are not so damaged that you are beyond help. Jesus came to heal the broken-hearted (see Luke 4:18).

The spirit of self-sabotage can be rooted in a fear of success. There is a psychological element involved in dealing with perpetual struggle. I have known families who built a culture around survival. Should someone be in trouble, sick, in the hospital, or facing hardship, they would gather together, cook big meals, and stay with the struggling soul continually. Yet their support system doesn't work as well with those who graduate from college, move away to a bigger city, or get a higher-level job. Under the surface, this becomes a fault line, and the tectonic plates start to shift as people struggle with the realization that they're more comfortable with failure than success because the family culture caters to trauma more effectively than achievement.

Sometimes, exposure to lifelong criticism by the people we hold dear, or the people we call successful, lies just under the surface until we find ourselves becoming who they said we'd become or avoiding the behaviors or identity they rejected or ridiculed. We don't want to bear the brunt of their criticism or become the ones our loved ones exclude, so we sabotage ourselves.

I still believe we can bounce back from self-imposed setbacks. If not, our hope would be small. All of us should be learning as we go and learning from our mistakes. Have you ever told yourself, "Don't do that," and then you just went right on and did it? Then, you had to say to yourself, "I knew I shouldn't have done that…" We've all been down that road.

People limit themselves and limit the miracle-working power of God because they believe in karma rather than sowing and reaping. These two things are not the same. Yin and yang is a balance, but it's not a biblical balance. A false balance is an abomination in the eyes of God (see Proverbs 11:1). Yin and yang is not a commensurate measure of good and evil. That's not the way God wants it to be. When grace is put on the scales, I don't get what I deserve! Grace outweighs me – immeasurably!

Some things are caused by the enemy and some things are caused by other human beings. Some were before you were saved, some after you were saved. But, there is still a power to rebuild. I have watched families and couples on the edge of breaking up, many times because of their own decisions, enter into a real crisis moment and come out on the other side of it better than they were when they went into it. The situation and the crisis made them confront issues they never would have talked about or dealt with otherwise. I have seen people go through financial calamity and the pressure they bounced back from caused them to change how they were handling their money.

Just because it was self-imposed doesn't mean you don't have the power to bounce back from it! If you made the decision that caused it, you can make the decision to get back out of it. If it was beyond your control, that would be one thing, but you have the power to choose to be resilient.

Trusted with Trouble

If you have hope that you'll bounce back, you can be trusted with trouble. None of us plans for trouble or goes looking for it, but God still allows us to experience it. When God knows He can trust us with trouble, He knows He can give us a bounce-back. Look at these words of Jesus to Simon Peter in Luke 22:31-32. It reads, "Satan has desired to sift you as wheat. But, I have prayed for you, that your faith may not fail. And when you have turned back, strengthen your brothers." In other words, when he bounced back! Jesus was trying to tell Simon that the enemy cannot get to him without a requisition, but that He was going to trust him with this trouble because He needed for him to go through something. He was going to pray that his faith wouldn't fail, not that he wouldn't have tears, or that he wouldn't have trouble, or that it wouldn't be an awkward season. When Simon Peter bounced back, he would receive the power to strengthen his brothers. Jesus was going to use him to strengthen someone else.

You don't have the power to say things you have no experience behind. I know you read two books and three scriptures on marriage, but if you haven't been married, it's not that the Bible isn't right, it's that you don't have the power to teach me how to be married. I know you understand that the Bible tells us to train up a child in the way he should go, but if you don't have kids, you don't have the moral authority to tell me how to raise children. So, if Jesus needs us to be able to minister to someone who's in a tough situation, He has to be able to trust us with some trouble! This is part of how we learn to stand in the gap! You're going to be able to find somebody else and say, "That was me. I've felt that way. I've been through that. But, if God can turn my situation around, He can turn yours around, too!" Even if you feel like you're in the middle of trouble now, Jesus is praying that your faith will not fail. Your bounce-back is on the way – God is going to bring you out!

The Proper Response

Let's consider Job. Chapter 1 of the book of Job introduces him as a man who was perfect and upright, fearing God and avoiding evil. Satan asked God, in verse 9, "Does Job fear you for nothing? For You have made a hedge around him on every side and have blessed the works of his hands." Now, Job was a man God could trust with trouble. His story shows us that we can come into a moment when we're being tested with a trial, and if we can keep our faith during our trouble and guard our tongue, not allowing it to sabotage our comeback, we'll bounce back.

Have you ever noticed that Job was minding his own business and God picked a fight for him? God said to Satan, in verse 8, "Have you considered him?" I want to focus on the part where Satan asks, "Does Job serve you for nothing?" There are a few things you need to know about this. The test will prove that Job is not serving God just because his hands are blessed, he's not serving God just because he's increasing, and he's not even serving God because he has a hedge. Job is serving God because He's God.

I believe in blessing and increase, but God doesn't want you serving that. And the enemy believes this is why Job is serving God. We can get so caught up in the story that we miss the point that there is a hedge! Perhaps this indicates that there was a time when Satan was trying to get to Job and realized there was a hedge around him – and not only around Job, but around everything he had. I want you to know that there is this hedge that you can't see with the natural eye. When this hedge is around you, God stands watch over what He's put into your life. He watches over kids who are in another state. He watches over you when people are trying to swindle you out of your money. According to Jeremiah 1:12, He watches over His word to perform it in your life.

I believe the book of Job tells us why God chose to put a hedge around him. Job was blameless and a man of integrity. Upright. Everyone knew his word was good, and they knew what he stood for. He feared God and was a man of reverence. God isn't putting a hedge around you just because – He's looking for those who reverence Him. Job was such a man. He turned away from evil. God is not putting a hedge around you just because your grandmother took you to church. The Bible calls him the greatest of all the men in the East. In verse 5, it says Job sanctified his children, interceding for them and for the people. Job put his prayers and his offerings together. Job didn't run to the altar because something was wrong or start doing good because he got tired of doing bad. God's intention was to prove that people don't just serve Him because of these things, but because of Who He is.

If you can hold your tongue and keep your praise in the middle of trouble, you will have a bounce-back. You can't afford to get in the middle of trouble and start blaming God and saying anything you want to say, losing your peace and your praise. You will get stuck if you do that. Notice that Job got the worst news of his life but responded with worship.

Especially when we're in the midst of shaking, we can't afford to lose our minds and turn against God. We know that God will bring us anything necessary for our destiny, so if He has allowed something to go, it has His vote that it's not necessary. We don't have to have it to get to where we're going if we still have our faith. Continuing with Job, it says in verse 22 that Job neither sinned nor charged God foolishly. Job's response was, in effect, "If we serve God in the good times, can we not also serve Him in the bad times?"

When Job's three friends heard what had happened, they came to mourn with him and comfort him. They each had their own theory of why he was in such a dire situation. We've covered much about the necessity of a good support network and close relationships, but can I tell you that you don't need friends like this? One said that Job's pride brought him into his trouble. One said he must have done something wrong. It doesn't really help when you're going through trouble for people to try to point out things like this.

Job walked through this situation and then God gave him

his bounce-back. Job 42 (40 chapters and a whole lot of life later!) records that God blessed the latter end of Job more than his beginning. God gave him twice as much as he had! God didn't just give him back what he had, He trusted Job with a double portion.

Maybe you feel like you're in a similar situation. But, if you will keep your integrity, if you will keep your praise, if you will keep your faith, God is going to give you double for your trouble and you're going to be able to be a blessing to someone else along the way. Jesus is praying that your faith will not fail and, when you have your rebound, you will use it to strengthen someone else.

Hang onto your integrity. Hang onto your reverence for God. Keep your hand over your mouth, if you have to, to keep from sabotaging your future. When you're going through something tough, sometimes you have to learn to be still and keep your peace. In those times when it seems like nothing is making sense around you, remember these words of Job in 1:21, "Blessed be the name of the LORD." Remember that David said it this way in Psalm 34:1, "I will bless the LORD at all times..."

We have to learn to bless Him on good days and bad days – when we're feeling stable and when we're surrounded by devastation, when people celebrate us and when people are hateful toward us. Our praise is not dependent on how others feel about us; it's based on how God feels about us and how we feel about God! You'll always have people who love you and people who hate you. You'll never have everyone on the same side, so you ought to learn to thank God – not for all things, but in all things.

I can be in the middle of something and not know if it's self-imposed, if it's enemy-imposed, or if it's God testing me, but I have learned that I can bless the Lord at all times. When I don't have all the answers figured out, I can still bless the Lord.

Built to Withstand

The road of life we travel is filled with twists and turns. Very seldom do things work out the way we plan. I believe we should have plans and a certain degree of organization to what we're doing, but the truth is that life does not always work out according to our charts. There are seasons in life that we have to navigate, but I'm concerned that modern Christianity has not prepared people for hardship. We need to know that we're not going to be skipping and grinning and laughing every day. If you mix up the God of the Bible with popular culture, it becomes easy to avoid the difficult things in life.

It's easy to develop idealism rather than realism – focusing on the ideal rather than dealing with the real. In the ideal world, everyone is nice, but in the real one, everyone is not. In an ideal world, everything works out. But, in the real world, it may not. In an ideal world, all your prayers get answered. But, in the real world, you don't always get what you thought you were going to get. It doesn't take long to realize you don't always get what you want, when you want it.

God is not interested as much in your comfortability as He is in getting His investment out of you. If you don't understand how to deal with hardship and the seasons of life and moments of disappointment, you're not going to be well-rounded. You'll be like the kids who were never told "No" and who always got what they wanted, who turn into adults who are very difficult to deal with!

We have so many fair-weather Christians because no one ever told them how to deal with hardship. Somebody skipped over the lessons on enduring hardness as a good soldier, that you have to endure sound doctrine, and that you have to be able to bounce back. You have to be able to recover from a hit and regain your momentum. You have to be able to recover from bad news and keep your praise in the midst of trouble. You have to be resilient.

I grew up in church, so I was always around two or three generations of people at the same time. The older people knew how to get through and that when you were in the middle of trouble, you didn't need to stay away from church, you needed to stay in! They knew how to endure hardness. These were the kind of people who believed they could pray and tell God they needed a word, believing that God would speak a word through the preacher just for their situation, preaching victory to them. They knew how to press in! They believed it mattered who they sat with, knowing they needed to be around people who could help them praise their way to their answer. I grew up around people who would change seats to get near those kinds of people (or to get away from the wrong ones!).

Mark 5:25 tells the familiar story of a certain woman who had an issue of blood for 12 years, who pushed past the crowd, saying within herself that if she could just touch the hem of Jesus' robe, she would be made well. Knowing virtue had gone out of Him, Jesus turned to her and told her that her faith had made her whole. She pressed in to find Jesus and, through her faith, received wholeness.

The danger with only experiencing prosperity is that it can make you soft. You become so addicted to favor that you don't know how to deal with persecution. In life, you'll have both!

If we're not careful, though, we'll raise up the next generation on such a diet of "ease" that they won't understand how to be prepared for hardship. When the enemy hits, because they're soft, they'll think the answer is to stay home for a month, rather than learning how to press in and get to Jesus.

Christianity was not born in the confines of comfort. It was born in a manger, surrounded by controversy. It was born with Herod trying to kill the children, in turning over tables, in temptation in the wilderness, and it was purchased with nails and spears and an old rugged cross. Jesus said it would end in a crucifixion, but He also said, in effect, "Don't buy a tomb. *Borrow* one." He was not going to keep it, just use it, knowing that on the third day, He'd show us how to bounce back (see Luke 18:33)! Someone may be counting on your crucifixion, but Jesus has put in you a resurrection!

We're living in a world that has gone wild. Teen suicide, a heroin epidemic, scandals exposed every day, and all kinds of madness are seen on a daily basis. God has entrusted our churches to be the stewards over cities, and I believe we're living in a time when church people need to lead the way in showing the world how to have a bounce-back.

For too long, people have been fed a steady diet of "just smile every day and think happy thoughts and click your heels together and go over the rainbow." That's not the same Bible I'm reading. This is not showroom Christianity. I don't need to know what my faith will do in the showroom or what it looks like in the case. I need to know what it will look like covered in mud and what it will do when it has to go over a rocky road.

We are living in a world where everything is moving around us and we have to know how to put our feet down, and having done all to stand, keep standing. The Bible I read instructs us (in Ephesian 6:11) to put on the whole armor of God to overcome the wiles of the devil. It says that there is a wrestling match, but it's not with flesh and blood – it's with principalities and powers. But, if you refuse to give up, you will win!

Some people haven't been taught how to bounce back, so instead, they backtrack. They never recover from a setback or a loss of momentum, from a bad decision or a sideways season, or from someone offending them. The distinction is what we do when we're in the middle of hardness or a setback – when we thought we were preparing for things to go one way, but they went another.

I knew a man when I was first starting in ministry who was coming down to about five years from retiring. Then, the plant he worked for closed and he lost everything. There he was, about 60 years old, given news that everything he had worked for was all gone. Rather than just feeling sorry for himself, he got one of his pickup trucks and started going to small businesses and restaurants, asking them if he could take over their trash collection. He got a few clients that way, and he set himself apart from his competitors because he would not only pick up all the trash, but he would also clean up the surrounding area. He did such a good job that word started to spread. He got enough business that he needed to get another truck. Then another one. Then, he started taking the salvageable things out of the trash and putting them in his barn, fixing them up and refurbishing them in his down time.

He eventually had a whole fleet of trucks and, once a year, he'd open up his barn and sell back the same items he had picked up from them! He has since passed away, but the last time I talked to him, he spoke about how he ended up with more at the latter end, saying it had looked like the end of the road for him, but he ended up with more than he would've had before the plant closed. He remarked that he never would've stepped out and done his trash collection and repair work if that first door had never shut!

I say that your bounce-back is in you because if you look back at the woman with the issue of blood that I referenced above, you see that she was not scheduled for a miracle. Jesus was not on His way to heal her. If you read the context, Jairus had a 12-year-old daughter who was sick and ready to die and she needed her own restoration. Jesus was on His way to this little girl. The woman, however, knew she had no other help. Jairus was interceding for his daughter and others were staying with her while he went to Jesus, but this woman had no one helping her. No one cleared the way for her. She was in this story by herself. She heard that Jesus was coming by and she said *to herself*, "If I can get to Jesus, if I just touch His clothes, I know I will be made well." She wasn't looking to someone else to do it for her.

This woman had a 12-year issue. She was dealing with a hemorrhage, she had spent all her money, and she was subject to many Levitical laws. This was affecting more than her physical or financial status. It affected her social status, her esteem, and her relationships. She was certainly not inactive. She had done what she knew to do. Whatever she had, she threw at this issue. But, rather than getting better, she got worse. With no help, no money, and an empty life, physically and emotionally spent, she arrived at the moment of desperation.

If you find yourself in moment of need and no one else is around, please know your bounce-back is in you. I believe life is better with others in our corner, but it is possible to find yourself alone. It would be great if other people were staying up at night praying for us, but the truth is that others may not care about our issues the same way we do. In those moments, go to God on your own behalf and ask Him to send help. Your bounce-back is in you and your help is on the way.

Let me say it this way – you would be surprised what you can achieve when you want it badly enough. When you really want something, you don't tolerate distraction. The people around this woman, between her and Jesus, are referred to as "the press." They were the mob, the crowd, and to her they were just a barrier to get through. She could not afford to be distracted by their opinions. Distraction is a sign that you're not focused, because when you are focused, you don't have time to be distracted. You can't lose your momentum every time someone has something to say. You can't lose your strength just because you didn't get the response you wanted from somebody else.

This woman said inside herself, "If I can just get to Jesus, if I can just touch His clothes…" Someone who had been hemorrhaging for 12 years was no doubt weak and anemic. It says that she came in from behind. If she came in from the front, they would have seen her and known she was unclean and probably tried to stop her. A comeback is coming from a behind position and sometimes it's the only option you have! Even with all the odds stacked against her, she still was able to initiate own bounce-back. Her actions and desperate faith got her through the crowd.

You can initiate your own restoration! You can create your own momentum! If you can get to Jesus, everything is getting ready to turn around. Other people can pray for us, which is certainly important, but we must find it on the inside of ourselves to get to Jesus and pull His virtue into our lives. He said that her faith had made her whole. She came to Him for healing, but she got wholeness! She not only bounced back, she bounced back better.

Redemption and Regeneration

The seed of everything is in itself. This is a Genesis principle and law. A thing is what a thing is. If we don't comprehend the origin and motivation of a thing, we have a tendency to act surprised when it shows us what it is. Wisdom, observation, and discernment allow us to know what a thing is and to make distinctions based on where a thing came from, its seed, and the direction it is headed. Jesus tells us that putting a new patch on an old garment is useless because they pull away from each other and that you can't put old wine into a new wineskin (see Mark 2:21-22). My takeaway is that some things are not compatible and are not designed to work together because they are what they are. Everyone cannot do everything, and every person is not compatible with every environment of life.

The first book of the Bible is Genesis. It is the DNA book, the beginning, the gene pool of everything. The beginning is very important to God. It starts in 1:1 with, "In the beginning, God…" In the same way, John 1 says, "In the beginning was the Word, and the Word was with God, and the Word was God." We have to understand the importance of the beginning, the foundation of something. If something starts wrong, it has the potential to stay wrong and end wrong. It may not look wrong for a while, but it will manifest itself at some point.

You could start something with the wrong motivation, like starting a relationship on lies or a business on deceit. You might begin a ministry based on rebellion, you could start a church because you split someone else's to get it, or you could marry someone who didn't belong to you – if you start it wrong, it has wrong in its seed. If wrong is in the seed, then it's going to show up somewhere, trust me on this. You can cover over it for a while, paint over it, and hang new shutters, but sooner or later the shaking will expose its faulty foundation. It is what it is – either it's built on a strong foundation or it's not!

The Bible teaches that for something to change, its genesis or "genes" have to change. It has to be re*gene*rated. It has to be redeemed, bought back, or restored. Adam was the gene pool for our humanity; his name shows us he did something to affect the human race. He is the genesis; he is the seed, the foundation, and the head of the earthly family. When God wanted to change it, He had to start a different head. He brought Jesus, "the last Adam" (according to 1 Corinthians 15:45), who re-generated us. We now have to identify ourselves, not based on what Adam did to us, but on what Jesus did for us! Adam gave us a setback, but Jesus gave us a bounce-back.

When God wanted to start a family of faith, He chose Abraham, who is referred to as the "father of faith" (see Romans 4:11). A father is a seed carrier. A father is one who is able to reproduce. Abraham is the father of nations. The seed is important. The gene pool is important. The foundation and where something comes from is important. God chose Abram, changed his name to Abraham, and determined that everything that would come through his loins would have the capacity to be blessed because of the blessing God put on him. God told him to leave the land of his father to a new land He would show him. He said He would make his name great, blessing those who blessed him and cursing those who cursed him. The beginning of the family of faith is in this man having a blessing spoken over his life.

Remember that, according to Galatians 3:29, we are Abraham's seed and heirs according to the promise. That means we are blessed coming in and going out, the head and not the tail, and so on - every promise of Abraham's can be ours, too. Just like your eyes, skin, hair, and height came through your natural DNA, when you tap into the life of faith, the blessing in your spiritual DNA pulses through your veins. It's *in* you to be blessed; the seed of blessing is your new beginning.

It's in your spiritual DNA to rebuild and be restored. It's not just some kind of motivational speech that someone came up with. The Bible tells us in 1 Peter 1:23 that we have been born of incorruptible seed. We are a part of the family of God. Jesus went to the tomb and bounced back! He got up of His own accord – that means it's on the inside of us to do it! Resurrection is part of who we are.

Look at the lineage of Abraham – he had Isaac, who then fathered Jacob, who had the sons who became the twelve tribes. This includes Joseph, who was sold into slavery in Egypt but bounced back to become a great leader and changed history. It then led onto Moses, who became the great deliverer of the children of Israel. Most of us are familiar with the stories, but I want you to see that Abraham's story is the genesis.

Abraham was different from his nephew Lot. Lot went with Abraham (whether he was invited or not is not clear), and he and his family were blessed because they were with Abraham. There is no doubt that people in your life are blessed because they are connected to you – and they may not even know it! The blessing caused the families of Abraham and Lot to multiply, but they became so many that strife arose between their herdsmen. Abraham was so blessed that he didn't have to fight Lot. He knew strife would short-circuit the blessing and the blessing was more important than being right. Abraham gave Lot the option of choosing whichever way he wanted to go. Lot, not being a man of faith, but of human outlook, chose the well-watered plains. It's amazing how sometimes the people you have helped and are blessed because of you turn around, leave you in the desert, and choose a better place for themselves! Lot left Abraham with the desert and chose the greener plains. But, because Abraham carried the seed of the blessing, he found water in the desert.

The place Lot chose became known as the twin cities of Sodom and Gomorrah, and most of us are familiar with the issues that came out of there. Abraham went to rescue Lot, but it was a pretty vile situation. Basically, without getting into too much detail, it shows us that Lot is very different than Abraham. Remember, a thing is what a thing is. If you get Abraham and Lot mixed up, you're in trouble. Eventually, Lot and his wife and daughters got out, but his wife looked back at the city, after being told not to, and was destroyed. Lot and his daughters ran off and began an incestuous relationship. It was in their DNA – origin matters! The Bible is so detailed about who begat so-and-so because it means something. The relationship that Lot had with his daughters resulted in the births of Ammon and Moab. From that seed and from that defilement came the archenemies of the people of Abraham. Every time you find Ammonites and Moabites, they are at odds with Abraham's seed.

Abraham developed a city called Bethlehem in Judah. Bethlehem means "the house of bread" and Judah means "praise." This was a city that meant, "the house of bread and praise." It was eventually the place where Jesus was born (fitting for the Bread of Life!). In Ruth 1, we find Elimelech and his wife Naomi, who were fortunate enough to live in this city, the house of bread and praise. They were just enjoying life with their two sons when a famine hit the land, so Elimelech took Naomi and their two sons to sojourn to Moab. He and his sons died, but Naomi arose with her daughters-in-law to return from Moab because the people in Bethlehem-Judah had bread.

This shows us that we have to be careful what we do when we hit a famine. A famine reveals things that abundance does not. A famine will test you and prove you. A famine is the lack of something, and it can be in any area: a lack of money, strained family relationships, lack of employment, or lack in your psychological or emotional health. When you feel like you are lacking in something, you have to be very careful what you do and how you deal with it.

Elimelech picked up his family and they left the house of bread and praise because of their famine. Guess where they went? They went to Moab. They didn't know the principle that a thing is what it is, that the seed of something tells you what it is. They left a place named after bread that was in famine, and they went to a place birthed out of wild, undisciplined, crazy, ugly, rebellious, unsubmitted relationships and people.

Sadly, they ended up in Moab and Elimelech died. Things die in Moab. Then, they stayed another 10 years and both sons married Moabite women. The only way to change DNA is with seed, but everything in this family that could bear seed was dead. All that remained were wombs, but the wombs were in Moab.

Somewhere in the middle of her famine, Naomi heard that the LORD had provided bread – and where would that exist other than the house of bread? There they were in Moab, but the bread they needed was in Bethlehem. She chose wisely and bounced back in the direction of bread and praise. She told her two daughters-in-law, Orpah and Ruth, that their husbands were dead and they could do whatever they wanted to do. Orpah chose to stay in Moab, but Ruth said to her, "Where you go, I will go. Your God will be my God, your people will be my people. Where you die, I will die" (see Ruth 1:16). Ruth had never known anything but Moab, but somehow, she knew that her bounce-back was in her. So, they went back together.

Can I tell you that one of the greatest ways you can begin to rebuild is to reconnect yourself with the house of bread and praise? I know that people fall out with God and fall out of fellowship with the local church for various reasons, but most of the time, people fall out when they experience famine and lack. You have to be careful with whom you join yourself in these times, because the principle governs. If famine is in the seed, if it's out of order, if dysfunction is in it, then that's what will develop and grow. It will not be redeemed, renamed, restored, or regenerated – it will stay what it is.

In the remainder of the Book of Ruth, we find that Ruth went back to bread and praise, but she didn't know anyone there. It turned out that Naomi had a relative in the area named Boaz, referred to as a kinsman redeemer. He was famous, rich – and single. Ruth gleaned from the fields and Boaz noticed her and eventually invited her into the house. Long story short, we find that Ruth positioned herself next to Boaz and he decided to marry her. The custom was that he had to first "redeem" her and Naomi and, in doing so, make a big proclamation in front of everyone. Naomi bounced back, even better than when she had left!

Let's consider for a moment, too, what would have happened if Naomi had never left in the first place. It was her husband Elimelech who chose Moab and, due to the culture of that time, she was not in a position of power to make her own decision. Someone else made a choice and she became the victim. Maybe you wouldn't have made a certain decision, but someone over you did, and now you find yourself, like Naomi, in a place where dreams begin to die. There is still hope for redemption!

When Ruth and Boaz got married, they gave birth to a son named Obed. Obed then had a son named Jesse, then Jesse had a son named David. Now, that's how you bounce back better! God took them out of famine and Ruth ended up in the lineage of Jesus! Jesus is in the line of Abraham (the father of faith) and David (the king of praise) because this woman jumped up out of famine. God will cause your latter end to be greater than your former end because it is His plan for you to bounce back better. It doesn't matter who did it to you or if you did it to yourself. Before God is done working with you, your rebound will come.

If you are in a sideways season, real change can occur if you come back to your senses and return to the house of bread and praise. It's time to shake it off and let everything standing in your way know that you may have taken a hit, but you are getting back up. You may have been knocked down, but not knocked out. It may have hurt and shaken you to your core, but it couldn't destroy your faith and praise. As long as you have those, you will bounce back!

The very fact that God preserved you means your bounce-back is on the way. If you are still standing and breathing God's beautiful air, then it's right there inside of you, ready to go.

Your famine could be foreclosure, divorce, children who walked away, molestation, psychological abuse, drug addiction, loss of a loved one, or a situation that doesn't make any sense. You might feel like you are dead and buried, but you have to know that the seed of resurrection is in you. Ruth changed her gene pool by receiving seed from the house of bread and praise and so can you. Your praise will release the bread of God in your life. You are going to bounce back better, stronger, healthier, happier, more fulfilled, and more in the will of God because the seed of the resurrection life of Jesus is within you.

My prayer is that the thoughts that led to this writing find a soft place in your heart so that as it gets rooted and grows and that it will help you navigate through tough days of personal famine or lack in your life. God has placed His Spirit inside of you, and it's a spirit that cannot be destroyed or overcome by any means. If any man be in Christ, he is a new creation (see 2 Corinthians 5:17). When you are in Christ, you have resurrection power flowing through you. You have redemption and regeneration inside of you. You will rebuild, reestablish, and be restored. It is the will of God for your life.

FINAL THOUGHTS

The lessons we learn in life serve us well. Some of them are expensive, but the experiences, both good and bad, add up to uniquely position us to help others.

If you're reading these closing words, it means you are a survivor. After all of the many tremors in life, you are still here, you are still breathing, and there is still something for you to do. Without contradiction, I believe that someone is waiting for you to bounce back and be the best you that you could possibly be.

Having been a recipient of the grace of God and the help of others, may you now have the power and the patience to restore your brothers and sisters, and help those you find by the wayside to rebuild – on solid ground.

GET THE FAULT LINES
STUDY GUIDE

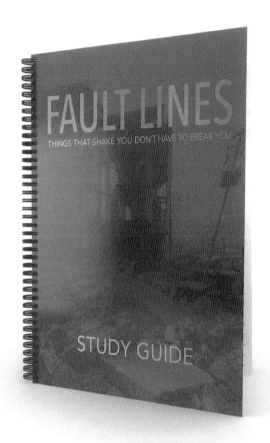

AVAILABLE ON WWW.MICHAELPITTS.COM

RESOURCES
AVAILABLE ON MICHAELPITTS.COM

BOOKS
Power Shifters
Boundary Shifters
Don't Curse Your Crisis
Breaking the Assignment of Spiritual Assassins
Soul Ties
Living on the Edge
Heal the World

SERIES
The Mystery of Power (MP3, DVD, CD)
The Mystery of Dominion (MP3, DVD, CD)
Bounce Back Better (MP3, DVD, CD)
The Commanded Blessing (MP3, DVD, CD)
The Mystery of Faith (MP3, DVD, CD)
Cycles (MP3, DVD, CD)
...and many more

MUSIC
Heal the World (CD, Digital Download)
Pierce the Darkness (CD, Digital Download)